Why I BELIEVE the Bible

"Dr. Burrell's sermons warm the heart and cheer the spirit." – *Church Standard*

Register This New Book

Benefits of Registering*

- ✓ FREE **replacements** of lost or damaged books
- ✓ FREE **audiobook** *Pilgrim's Progress*, audiobook edition
- ✓ FREE information about new titles and other **freebies**

www.anekopress.com/new-book-registration

*See our website for requirements and limitations.

Why I BELIEVE the Bible

REASONABLE AFFIRMATION THAT
EVERYTHING IN THE BIBLE IS TRUE

DAVID JAMES BURRELL

We love hearing from our readers. Please contact us at www.anekopress.com/questions-comments with any questions, comments, or suggestions.

Why I Believe the Bible
© 2022 by Aneko Press
All rights reserved. Published 2022.
All rights reserved. First edition 1917.
Revisions copyright 2022.

Please do not reproduce, store in a retrieval system, or transmit in any form or by any means – electronic, mechanical, photocopying, recording, or otherwise, without written permission from the publisher. Please contact us via www.AnekoPress.com for reprint and translation permissions.

Scripture quotations from The Authorized (King James) Version. Rights in the Authorized Version in the United Kingdom are vested in the Crown. Reproduced by permission of the Crown's patentee, Cambridge University Press.

Cover Designer: Jonathan Lewis
Editors: Sheila Wilkinson and Ruth Clark

Aneko Press
www.anekopress.com
Aneko Press, Life Sentence Publishing, and our logos are trademarks of
Life Sentence Publishing, Inc.
203 E. Birch Street
P.O. Box 652
Abbotsford, WI 54405

RELIGION / Christian Theology / Apologetics
Paperback ISBN: 978-1-62245-778-6
eBook ISBN: 978-1-62245-779-3
10 9 8 7 6 5 4 3 2 1
Available where books are sold

Contents

Foreword vii

Ch. 1: The Antecedent Presumption 1

Ch. 2: The Claim: Is It Verified? 5

Ch. 3: An Unaccountable Unity 13

Ch. 4: Its Completeness 19

Ch. 5: Its Sufficiency 23

Ch. 6: Its Literary Value 31

Ch. 7: Its Up-to-Dateness 45

Ch. 8: Its Tone of Authority 53

Ch. 9: Its Trustworthiness 59

Ch. 10: Its Influence on Personal Life 63

Ch. 11: Its Influence on National Life 73

Ch. 12: Its Place in the Forefront of Events 79

Ch. 13: It Is Christ's Book 91

Ch. 14: Excursus: A Hypothetical Story 105

Ch. 15: It Is the Church's Book 113

Ch. 16: It Is Everybody's Book 121

Ch. 17: Its System of Doctrine 127

Ch. 18: Its Moral Code 133

Ch. 19: Its Plan of Salvation 141

Ch. 20: Its Enemies 145

Ch. 21: Its Indestructibility 159

Afterword 165

David James Burrell – A Brief Biography 175

Other Similar Titles 183

This book
Is dedicated to
Our old-fashioned mothers
Who, with all their knowing,
"Just know their Bibles true,"
And live that way.

Foreword

A boy who had been dedicated to the ministry at birth and constantly reminded of that fact by a devoted mother, left home at sixteen to prepare himself for the work before him. As he was exposed to the adverse winds of current unbelief, he drifted from the moorings of faith little by little until, at the conclusion of his college course, he found himself without chart or compass on an open sea.

The choice of a profession was then before him. Not without an inward struggle, he resolved to enter upon a theological course in the hope of regaining a sufficient measure of faith to warrant his going on. It was a foregone conclusion that the experiment would fail. No man in such a quicksand can recover his footing by a dead lift, anymore than a planet, which has swerved from its orbit, can automatically save itself from exile in infinite space.

Those were dreary years, four miserable years of evasion, compromise of conscience, and vain efforts to travel in "the middle of the road." It was a hopeless case. There is no middle of the road. If Christ was not what he claimed to be but was only a man, justly condemned to death for *making himself equal with God;* if the Bible is not what it claims to be but is a mere book among books to be laughed out of court for assuming to have been written *by holy men of God . . . as they were moved by the Holy Spirit;* if the manger and the cross and the open sepulcher are to be explained away as figments of the imagination without basis in fact or any practical bearing on the life here or hereafter, what need is there of the ministry or what excuse can be offered for entering it?

So the young man reasoned within himself that with all the avenues of strenuous life open before him, he would obviously be a fool to choose a ministry without a message, and a scoundrel to assume vows which were better kept in the breach than in the observance. Thus doubting and questioning, this candidate for holy orders stood at the crossing of the ways.

Just then he was unexpectedly called to minister at a deathbed. An old Scotsman, who had been trained at a Highland fireside but had wandered far from the landmarks of truth and righteousness, was looking into the dark with frightened eyes. All night long he kept saying, "Tell me how to face God! Is there a God? Was Christ his only begotten Son? Did he die for me? Can his blood cleanse from all sin? Read me what the Bible says about it. But wait; is the Bible true? They say it's no better than any other book. What do you think? Man, I am dying! Don't trifle now. Tell me."

All night long! Put yourself in the place of that young man. What would you have done? At daybreak he found himself on his knees, humbled and put to shame by the manifest intervention of a loving God. In trying to tell a sinner how to die, he had discovered how to live. At daybreak, by the side of the dead, the living stood up and praised God.

The doorway into the ministry was now open before him. With Christ as his Savior and the Bible as an infallible rule of faith and conduct, he could assume the vows of his ordination with the clear conscience of an honest man. He had his message to deliver as an ambassador of Christ, a message involving the issues of eternal life. Whether he would preach or not was no longer an open question; he must preach, because he had something to say, something worthwhile, something with the sanction of a *Thus saith the* LORD behind it.

Half a century has passed since these things happened. The young preacher in the meantime has attended many deathbeds and ministered to multitudes of the living, and he has never wavered in his conviction that Christ is faithful and that the Bible is a dependable book to live by and die by.

Chapter 1

The Antecedent Presumption

If I regarded Scripture as a mingled tissue of truth and falsehood, or as merely containing a more or less small portion of truth, I could not as an honest man say that I believe it. But I do believe it, and I mean precisely what I say. To my mind, the Bible is not true in spots, but is true and trustworthy from beginning to end.

And this is the historic faith of the Christian church all through the ages. The enemies of the Bible make so much noise at times that old-fashioned believers are moved to lament as Elijah did under the juniper tree: *[They] have forsaken thy covenant, thrown down thine altars, . . . and I, even I only, am left* (1 Kings 19:10). But battles are not won with wind instruments, and neither faith nor reason builds its altars under juniper trees. There are multitudes in Israel who have not bowed their knees to Baal. The shouting and the tumult cease, but truth and righteousness fight on to certain victory in the long run.

It is a great thing to be a conservative, not inactively like reservoirs of still water, but progressively like rivers that keep within their banks while rolling on toward the sea. We are bound to move with the moving world, providing we do not move away from the immovable faith which was *once delivered unto the saints* (Jude v. 3). We must keep an open house for truth, but by the same token we are bound to double-bolt our doors when falsehood knocks and cries, "Let me in!"

Whether a man believes his Bible or rejects it, two things may be required of him. On the one hand, he must frankly and truthfully state his position without mumbling or murmuring; and on the other hand, he must be able to always give an answer to every man that asks him a reason for it.

There is something to be said, before we go a step further, about the reasonableness of looking for a revelation of some sort. This, while it proves nothing, will prepare the way for positive propositions further on.

The presumption runs like this: *If there is a God anywhere in the universe, and if that God is our Father, he would certainly not leave us in doubt as to the great problems involved in the issues of eternal life.*

If it is reasonable to expect an earthly father to comfort his children in distress by assuring them of his wise purposes for them, our Father in heaven would certainly do no less (Matthew 7:11).

If a caring king puts up signs to guide wayfarers through the dense forests and along the perplexing roads of his domain, the King of Kings would assuredly not leave his subjects to wander at their wits' end.

Plato lamented that he was adrift upon a raft with no rudder at hand or guiding star before him; yet even he, pagan though he was, risked the hope that the gods would sometime "give us a good staunch boat to sail in." This was the expression of a universal instinct. Assuming a god, it would appear that somewhere there must be a clear and distinct revelation not only of himself but also of his compassionate plans and purposes concerning us.

So much for the previous presumption. We shall now consider the claim of the Bible itself to be precisely such a revelation as would be expected of a just and loving God.

Chapter 2

The Claim: Is It Verified?

The claim of the Bible is threefold, and it is expressed in no uncertain terms.

First: The Bible claims to be inspired and does not leave the least possible doubt as to what it means by "inspiration." The word is *theopnustia:* literally, "breathed of God" (2 Timothy 3:16).

I breathe upon a window on a frosty morning and leave a lacework picture there of turreted palaces and landscapes and armies marching to battle with diamond-pointed spears. So God once breathed through human lips upon a series of parchments, which are called the Scriptures. The deposit left on those original parchments was the very breath (*pneumo*) of God. Therefore it must have been inerrant truth, since it is unthinkable that God should breathe a lie.

Second: The Bible claims to be inspired in a definite and singular way. Namely, *the prophecy came not in old time by the will of man: but holy men of God spake as they were moved* [or borne onward] *by the Holy [Spirit]* [*pneuma,* "the breath"] of God (2 Peter 1:21).

It thus appears that the sacred writers were something more than mere amanuenses (those who are employed to write or copy what another dictates or writes). While free to express the divinely revealed truth in their own words and according to their own mental processes, they were so inspired by the Holy Spirit that they were safeguarded on the one hand against all possible error, and directed on the other into a clear statement of truth precisely as God would have it.

Third: This singular claim is made for all Scripture, for it is written, *All scripture is given by inspiration of God, and is profitable for doctrine, for reproof, for correction, for instruction in righteousness: that the man of God may be perfect, thoroughly furnished unto all good works* (2 Timothy 3:16-17).

In other words, there can be no picking and choosing from among the Scriptures, as when one orders a dinner *a la carte*, saying, "I like this," and "I do not care for that." The table is divinely spread, and all its delicacies are nutritious, not all alike or equal for building up the same parts and processes of life, but some for doctrine, others for reproof and correction, still others for instruction in righteousness. None are without distinct and definite uses.

The words quoted from 2 Timothy 3 bear little further examination. They were addressed to the young pastor of the Christian church in Ephesus. He was surrounded by diverse temptations. Ephesus was the chief commercial center for a considerable portion of the trade of Asia, a resort for fashionable people who wished to lose themselves in the whirl of vicious indulgence, and a distinguished seat of pagan learning. The young pastor had, therefore, to meet all the allurements common to the prevalent custom of sordid business, carnal pleasure, and worldly wisdom. But against these he was fortified by the training which he had received not merely from Paul, his spiritual foster father, but also from his mother, Eunice, and from another elect lady, his grandmother Lois. By these he had been instructed in *the holy scriptures, which are able to make [men] wise unto salvation* and to encourage them for the stress of daily life (2 Timothy 3:15).

In this letter of Paul's, full of faithful counsel and admonition, he directed the young minister to be mindful of the foundation of faith and morals which had thus been imparted to him: *Continue thou in the things which thou hast learned and hast been assured of* (2 Timothy 3:14).

How many a youth in the hurly-burly of metropolitan life has need of similar counsel in these days! Never in the history of the world has there been a time when the young and unwary were confronted by temptations more alluring than now. The life of commerce makes its distracting claims, and the life of pleasure beckons from doorways and windows along the way. Presumptuous folly, arrayed in the garb of wisdom, stands at the corners of the streets, crying aloud that the old truths are outdated, that the Bible is untrustworthy, that religion is but a refined form of superstition, and that the spirit of the age is more important than the Spirit of God.

Now let the hallowed past rise to help and strengthen. Let memory recall the voice of the dear mother who, as Cowper says, "just knew, and knew no more, her Bible true!"[1] Let the voice of the village preacher, far away in the glamor of the vanished past, be heard again, commending the cross, the old-fashioned Book, and the precepts of a holy life.

Oh men and women, let us continue in the things which we have learned and been assured of. Why should we be swept from our moorings by every contrary wind of destructive teaching? Let us stand by our principles if we have any. Let us conform to our convictions. So shall the truths that have proved themselves to the thoughtful world for centuries be ours to serve as an anchor of our souls, both sure and steadfast, taking hold of that which is within the veil. Unless we are fully persuaded

---

[1] William Cowper, "Truth," *Poems: by William Cowper, of the Inner Temple,* Line 327, 1782.

that our ancestors were simple folk and that the church of the centuries has been imposed on by a system of *cunningly devised fables,* it is needful to respect the ancient landmarks and, chief among them, the Bible. To abandon that is to be without an anchor in the storm, adrift upon an open sea.

But the question now confronts us: Does the Bible verify its claim?

Suppose we treat that question precisely as if it were pending in a court of justice. The evidence is to be submitted to a jury of fair-minded men. Two things are necessarily assumed at the outset. One is that the minds of these jurymen shall be clear of prejudice. Otherwise, to proceed with the argument would be as hopeless as was Galileo's attempt to prove the existence of the moons of Jupiter to a body of inquisitors who refused to look through his telescope for fear they would have no case against him.

The other prerequisite on the part of these jurymen is that each shall do his own thinking. The jury system is rightly regarded as one of the necessary pillars of any commonwealth founded on the rights of man. It has been said, "The entire Constitution of England with its balances and complications and delicate adjustments was framed for the main purpose of impaneling twelve honest men and true." The business of the presiding judge is to hold the balances and interpret the law. The attorneys are bound by honor to argue the case on its merits. The witnesses are sworn to speak "the truth, the whole truth, and nothing but the truth." And the "twelve honest men and true" are directed to find a verdict in accordance with the law and evidence bearing on the matter in hand. The ideal is perfect, its object being to secure equal and impartial justice for all sorts and conditions of men.

In practice, however, the system does not always attain this end. It frequently happens that a jury cannot agree. There is a difference of opinion as to the application of the law or the weight of evidence in the case. The foreman advises the court accordingly, and he is instructed to return and inform his associates that they must agree. Then the majority argues with the minority and perhaps succeeds in persuading them – all but one. This stubborn fellow holds out. The result is a "hung jury," and the case is set for retrial or given up.

I sing the praises of that stubborn man. Many a life, trembling in the balance, has been saved by him. He is true to himself and to the right of the matter, as God helps him to see it. He does his own thinking, and declines to farm out his brain and conscience to others. He is a true man, an independent man, a necessary man, a mighty man.

His value has been approved in many of the great crises of history. In the beginning of the Christian church, a man of this character was needed to antagonize the false teachers who, under the leadership of Arius, attacked the deity of Christ. The man appeared in the person of Athanasius, the bishop of Alexandria, who was repeatedly exiled and ceaselessly persecuted for his unswerving devotion to reason and conscience. The errorists of the church were against him; the influence of many in ecclesiastical authority was against him; the power of the empire was against him. On being advised by certain of his friends that "the world was against him," he made the memorable reply, "Then I am against the world!" Who shall estimate the influence of that lone juror? The time-servers who weakened are forgotten, but *Athanasius contra mundum* (Athanasius against the world) is immortalized in the poetic justice of history. His monument is the Athanasian Creed, in which millions of Christians pay tribute to the heroism of one who would not "bow the pregnant hinges of his knees that thrift might follow fawning."[2] All honor to such men!

---

2   William Shakespeare, *Hamlet, Act III, Scene II,* 1609.

There has never been a time when the call for such independent thinkers was louder than right now. This is true not only in social and political affairs but also preeminently in the subject of religion. And behind all religious problems in this area is that of biblical authority, because if the Scriptures are not reliable, we have absolutely no ultimate standard by which to determine the truth or falsity of any religious thesis.

What we want, then, for the business immediately at hand, is a panel of unbiased and independent jurors. In other words, they must be honest doubters.

Let there be no mistake at this point, however; for many a man who thinks himself an honest doubter is in fact a confirmed and stubborn unbeliever. It has been said that doubt is either the agony of a noble soul or the frivolity of a fool. An honest doubter is one who, realizing the importance of a right settlement of an important issue, does not rest day or night until he arrives at the truth concerning it. He puts all preconceptions away and, with a clear conscience and a single purpose, addresses himself to the problem before him.

Is the reader thus prepared to examine the evidence? Is his mind free from bias and open to conviction? If not, he is promptly challenged because no amount of argument based on facts can enable him to pass an honest judgment on the merits of the case. If, however, he is sure of his unbiased sincerity in the serious quest of truth, he is competent to hear the evidence and pass on it.

One of the great discourses of Christ, in which he stated the authority of his teaching, is recorded in the seventh chapter of John. He was speaking on the porch of the temple to a company of people who were divided in their opinion concerning him. Some believed that his teaching was true and that he was what he claimed to be. Others, including the scribes and Pharisees, were so opposed to him that they were even then plotting to kill him. The Teacher himself put the case calmly and dispassionately before them in this way: *If any man will do his will, he shall know of the doctrine, whether it be of God* (John 7:17).

Are we willing to follow the direction of the divine will in order that we know whether the teaching is of God? If so, we may proceed with the hearing of the case; otherwise, we might as well call a halt here and now because "a man convinced against his will is of the same opinion still."[3]

---

[3] Samuel Butler, *Hudibras in Three Parts, Written in the Time of the Late Wars*, 1663, 1664, 1678.

Chapter 3

An Unaccountable Unity

It is difficult if not impossible to account for the singular unity of the Scriptures without crediting them to a divine origin.

Here is a volume made up of sixty-six books on a large variety of themes, composed by forty distinct writers of various tongues and nationalities, writing at intervals along a period of sixteen hundred years and representing all degrees of racial development from semi-barbarism to the highest degree of culture. Yet, strange to tell, when bound together, these sixty-six books constitute a harmonious and consistent whole, yielding one system of doctrine, one code of ethics, and one rule of faith and practice for all the children of men.

Shall we call this an accidental circumstance? The folly of such a statement would immediately be recognized in any other discipline. Consider forty distinct persons of different tongues and degrees of musical education who pass through the organ loft of a church at long intervals and, without any possibility of collusion, strike sixty-six notes, which yield the theme of an oratorio when combined. It is respectfully submitted that the man who regarded that as an accidental circumstance would by universal consent be regarded as – to put it mildly – sadly deficient in common sense. The conclusion from such a harmonious combination would be irrefutable: namely, that one controlling mind, and that of a great tone master, was behind it.

The Bible is in two volumes. The first of these is called the Old Testament and the second is the New Testament. In certain regions, there is a tendency to accept the latter while practically rejecting the former as having little or no value for modern readers. Not long ago in a convention of Sunday school teachers, a clergyman is reported to have said, "The Old Testament is out of date; let me have a few of the psalms and a chapter or two of Isaiah, and I have no further use for it." There are not many ministers or laymen, probably, who would be willing to speak so frankly, but an impression of this sort has gone abroad, and the consequent neglect of the Old Testament is so prevalent that a consideration of the subject in this connection may be profitable for us.

Let us affirm, therefore, that the Old Testament is not only an essential and inseparable part of the Bible, but that it also perfectly agrees and harmonizes with the New Testament. The plot of a connected story runs through both volumes: specifically, the story of the cross – so connectedly that no coherent or consecutive view of the divine plan of salvation can be gained without an understanding of both. The New Testament is woven into the Old Testament like the warp of a fabric into its woof, or to use the words of Augustine: "The New Testament is enfolded in the Old and the Old Testament is unfolded in the New."

The sum and substance of both volumes is briefly comprehended in the saying, *For God so loved the world, that he gave his only begotten Son, that whosoever believeth in him should not perish, but have everlasting life* (John 3:16).

The story opens at the gateway of Paradise where, at the moment when our first parents sinned against God, the first gospel was given: "The Seed of woman shall come in the fullness of time to bruise the serpent's head." The red trail of the atoning blood can be traced from there through all the pages of the Book. The plot thickens as we read through Chronicles and Psalms and prophecies. But with Israel's abandonment of the messianic hope, the lights in the temple go out, and the darkness deepens into an Egyptian night of four hundred years – a night which is broken by the shining of the star of Bethlehem and the angels' song: *Glory to God in the highest, and on earth peace, good will to men* (Luke 2:14).

By this it is evident that the "worthies" of the olden time were saved precisely as we are. The Old Testament, known as the Book of the Law, was a *schoolmaster to [lead them] unto Christ* (Galatians 3:24). The first sinner had an early indication of the Savior. The patriarchs *rejoiced to see [his] day*. The faithful who gathered around the brazen altar were sufficiently initiated into the mystery of the sacrificial Lamb of God. Such ancients as Abraham and David and Isaiah were believers as much as we are, but they looked forward to the sacrifice while we look backward to it as an accomplished fact.

The first volume of the Book is, indeed, a necessary key to the second. How shall we understand the words *Behold the Lamb of God* unless we are familiar with the tragic incident of the Passover and the prophetic ritual of the altar? How shall we comprehend the saying of Jesus to Nicodemus: *As Moses lifted up the serpent in the wilderness, even so must the Son of man be lifted up: that whosoever believeth in him should not perish, but have eternal life* (John 3:14-15) unless, like Nicodemus, we are familiar with the story of Ezion-geber? Thus, in order to enter the holy of holies, we must pass through the outer court.

The gospel in the New Testament glows with the light of the *most excellent glory* that shone above the tabernacle of the Old Testament. The mercy seat is sprinkled with the blood of

Calvary, and the open sepulcher in Joseph's garden echoes with ancient prophecies of life and immortality brought to light. The importance of studying the Old Testament is obvious if we desire to understand the full, broad, glorious significance of the divine plan of salvation from the penalty and power of sin.

As there is only one God, so there is only one authoritative Book of God, and the Bible is that one. Its parts all hold together as a coherent and consistent though complex unit, all being inspired and profitable for the making of a man.

It is not meant by this, however, that all portions of the Bible are equally profitable. The law with respect to the robbing of a bird's nest is obviously not as important as the precept *Thou shalt not kill*. It is not as essential that we should familiarize ourselves with the catalog of names in Genesis 10 – though this furnishes the basis of ethnological science – as that we should know the riches of divine grace. But there is a good and sufficient reason for every portion of it. Not a chapter is negligible or dispensable.

It is true also that much of the Bible is not designed to be read in the public services of the sanctuary or even at the family altar. In a book intended to touch life at every point in its circumference, there are many passages fit only for communication between a man and God alone – unveilings of carnal rottenness in the secret imaginations of the heart, flashes of a two-edged sword that cuts to the very dividing of the bones and marrow. These are to be read only in those private chambers where the soul sits bare and naked before God.

But the supremely important point to remember in the study of the Scriptures is that their core is the divine plan of salvation. Omit that and the whole fabric is reduced to threads and fringes. It is only with the cross as our golden key that we are able to enter the Bible to perceive not only the unity of its various parts, but also the profitableness of every part for some of the diverse uses of life. All Scripture is thus seen to contribute to the far-reaching purpose of God in our redemption and building up unto the measure of the fullness of the stature of a man.

Chapter 4

Its Completeness

The Bible is a comprehensive summary of all spiritual truth, as far as a knowledge of spiritual truth is necessary to our temporal and eternal well-being. It is characterized by Paul in one of his letters to Timothy where he says, *But continue thou in the things which thou hast learned and hast been assured of, knowing of whom thou hast learned them; and that from a child thou hast known the holy scriptures, which are able to make thee wise unto salvation through faith which is in Christ Jesus. All scripture is given by inspiration of God, and is profitable for doctrine, for reproof, for correction, for instruction in righteousness: that the man of God may be perfect, thoroughly furnished unto all good works* (2 Timothy 3:14-17).

It thus appears that, in the opinion of Paul, all spiritual truth, as far as needed for our guidance, is summarized in the Scriptures. This fact is worthy of emphasis in view of what is being said about "progressive revelation."

Do we affirm, then, that there is no such thing as progress in the understanding of truth? By no means! But we do insist that all progress in spiritual knowledge is within this Book. As John Robinson said, when bidding farewell to the Pilgrims who were embarking at Delft Haven, "I pray you to remember that new light will be ever breaking forth from the Word of God!" New light, ever, but no new Sun of Righteousness. It is a singular fact that, despite the philosophical research of centuries, no truth of spiritual things has ever been discovered beyond the boundaries of Scripture, so it would appear that Scripture contains the ultimate and adequate sum total required for the supply of human need. There are no limitations in God, but there is a definite limit to our knowledge of him.

There is no new force in the material universe, though there is no end of new adjustments and applications of force. While there are no new principles in the spiritual world, there are continually new interpretations and larger uses of them. The sun, which is our source of light and energy, is not changed to meet the demands of a progressive world, though there are many *new things under the sun*. The Bible, in like manner, though closed and sealed long centuries ago, was divinely adjusted to the progress of all succeeding ages.

The uninspired word *Finis* on the last page of the Bible is as true as though it were incorporated into it. The meaning of that word is that the revelation of truth contained therein is so comprehensive that there would never be need of an addendum. It stands like a challenge to the progress of the future, saying, "Supplant me or supplement me if you can!"

The last words of the last chapter of the last portion of Scripture are significant: *I testify unto every man that heareth the words of the prophecy [teaching] of this book, if any man shall add unto these things, God shall add unto him the plagues that are written in this book: and if any man shall take away from the words of the book of this prophecy, God shall take away his part out of the book of life, and out of the holy city, and from the things which are written in this book* (Revelation 22:18-19).

I am not unaware that those who deny the integrity of the

Scriptures are accustomed to saying that the warning referred to was intended to apply only to that particular portion of Scripture that contains it, namely, the *Book of the Revelation of John*. But this does not relieve the situation for two reasons: first, it is not easy to perceive the grounds upon which this limitation is based or how its originators discovered it; second, even granting it, they would probably be as reluctant (putting it mildly) to consent to the full inspiration and trustworthiness of John's account of his apocalyptic visions as of any other portion of the Bible. The only escape from the dilemma on their part is to deny the singular truth of the Scriptures *in toto*, which, frankly stated, is precisely what they do.

At this point, attention is called to a fact which is difficult to explain on the part of those so-called biblical experts who deny – and not infrequently deride – the plenary and inerrant inspiration of the original writings of Scripture. The business of textual criticism is to purge all current versions of unwarranted changes and additions by careful and scholarly comparison with the earliest manuscripts in order to arrive, as nearly as possible, at the original text. But why do this? If this Book is to be classed as mere literature and treated accordingly, why not seek for the latest edition instead of the first edition? The textbooks in use when we were children at school are all obsolete. Those now being studied by our boys and girls must presently be revised and brought up to date. The last editions are required in every case. Why, then, should the first edition of the Scriptures be in such universal demand? Isn't this a practical concession that the original manuscript of Scripture, if found, would prove to be the highest authority in spiritual things for this and every age? In other words, marvelous to tell, the Bible, written so many centuries ago, must have been intended to abide through all generations as an unalterable book because it is full and complete, measuring out to the entire race its supply for all moral needs from the beginning to the very end of time.

Chapter 5

Its Sufficiency

The Bible would not be a complete book if it did not supply all the moral and spiritual needs of all sorts and conditions of men.

Does it meet that requirement?

In the so-called parable of the rich man and Lazarus, we are given to understand that our Lord thought so. It goes like this: In a certain town there lived six brothers, all eminently respectable men. They obeyed the laws, paid their honest debts, and minded their own affairs. As to spiritual things, they were noncommittal; why should they trouble themselves about God and the future when they were so comfortable in the enjoyment of the world here and now? The worst that could be said of them was that they were living self-centered lives. But that was bad enough, as we shall see.

One of these brothers had a luxurious home where, clothed in purple and fine linen, he lived luxuriously every day. The fact that a certain beggar, sick and forlorn, was accustomed to sitting before his gate may have annoyed him, but he satisfied his conscience by giving the poor fellow the crumbs that fell from his table. He probably felt that he was magnanimous in not ordering him off the premises.

Now it came to pass in the course of events, that the beggar died, as all beggars do, and being a worthy man in spite of his poverty, he went to heaven. He was received into that innermost place of happiness, which the rabbis were accustomed to calling *Abraham's bosom,* a term borrowed from the custom of reclining on couches at banquets. By this we understand that his faithfulness admitted him to the near presence of the father of the faithful, where a feast of spiritual delicacies was spread before him.

And then in the course of events, the rich man also died. What? Yes, they all do. He died, and he was buried. No doubt he had a dignified funeral, and his virtues were commemorated in a glowing epitaph. What then? He went to his own place. Where else could he go but to the place for which his character suited him? That place is called *Sheol* in the Hebrew, and in our translation, a word not to be mentioned in polite ears. Yet Christ used it without mumbling. It is the place appointed for all sordid and selfish souls who live for self and die without God.

The two places thus designated were far apart, but the distance could not be measured in terms of space, for the rich man in hell could see what was transpiring in heaven and was within calling distance of it. Shall we wonder about this? Did you never know a husband and wife who, living under the same roof, were infinitely separated from each other by the fact that they were hopelessly at odds concerning vital things? So here, the rich man is represented as holding a conversation with Abraham, though he could not approach him.

Let it be observed that in this conversation he makes no complaint with respect to his own condition in the final adjustment of things. He was doubtless aware of the saying,

Whatsoever a man soweth, that shall he also reap, and apparently he recognized the fact that justice was being meted out to him (Galatians 6:7).

But he had a request to make: namely, that Lazarus might be sent, with a finger dipped in that water to cool his tongue, which was burning with thirst, the consuming thirst of vain regret for opportunities unheeded and gone by.

To grant that request was impossible in the nature of the case. The water that he craved was not among the "good things" which he had chosen and enjoyed in his lifetime. The Persians have a proverb: "The remembrances of past happiness are the wrinkles of the soul." What shall be said, then, of the remembrances of past privilege and lost opportunity?

And beside all this, said Abraham, *between us and you there is a great gulf fixed: so that they which would pass from hence to you cannot; neither can they pass to us, that would come from thence.* Who fixed that gulf? Not God, for it is written that the twelve gates of his heaven are wide open forever. Why, then, doesn't this rich man pass in? For the same reason that so many homeless, friendless, cheerless folk pass by our church doors without a thought of entering. However depressed their condition in the outer darkness, they are more comfortable there than they would be in a praying, psalm-singing company like ours.

Likewise with the rich man in the parable, nothing but his own choosing excluded him from the fellowship of saints. He hears them singing, *Holy, holy, holy,* Lord *God Almighty,* but to dwell surrounded by the praises of a holy God would be torture to him. He hears them praising the Savior in such glowing terms as these: "Worthy art thou to receive honor and glory and power and dominion, for thou hast washed our robes and made them white." But what does he care for Christ or for the righteousness of saints? He sees them going on their Lord's errands as ministering spirits, but he has never learned the generous pleasure of gracious deeds. Oh no, heaven would have been a more unbearable place than hell for one whose life of self-pleasing had so utterly disqualified him for it. He was thirsty, but not for water like that. He was unhappy, but not with any longing for the jubilation of saints. What he wanted was not a change of character but merely a lessening of pain. His choice had been made in his earthly life and was still made. He would not choose otherwise. The gulf was fixed, and he himself had fixed it. His character had been crystallized by death, which is the end of probation, for it is written, *He that is unjust, let him be unjust still: . . . and he that is holy, let him be holy still* (Revelation 22:11). And what could change it?

He had, however, another request to make: *I pray thee therefore, father, that thou wouldest send [Lazarus] to my father's house: for I have five brethren; that he may testify unto them, lest they also come into this place of torment* (Luke 16:27-28). By this we understand that his brothers were still living in the selfish enjoyment of wealth and sensual comfort and without troublesome thoughts of death or of that which follows it. There is an indication in this request that, in the opinion of the rich man, they were not getting a fair chance. It is as if he said, "My brothers do not know! If they were sufficiently informed as to the reality of eternal things, they would surely change their manner of life."

But would they? Now consider the answer, for here is where the sufficiency of Scripture comes in. The answer was, *They have Moses and the prophets; let them hear them* (Luke 16:29).

The term *Moses and the prophets* was one of the current phrases used to designate the Scriptures. The indication is that these brothers had in the Bible all the light that was necessary for their guidance and admonition.

At this point the rich man protests, *Nay, father Abraham: but if one went unto them from the dead, they will repent* (Luke 16:30).

This sounds reasonable, but in fact there was nothing in it. The time came when one did actually rise from the dead – when Christ himself, who had been crucified before their eyes, came forth from his sepulcher, as was certified by the Scriptures that *he was seen of above five hundred brethren at once* – and still we are left to believe that they were unconvinced and went on living in the same way (1 Corinthians 15:6).

So comes the final word: *If they hear not Moses and the prophets, neither will they be persuaded, though one rose from the dead* (Luke 16:31). Here is the climax of the parable. It has pleased God to reveal himself in the Scriptures as a God of infinite justice and infinite love. He has made himself known in this manner so that sinners might repent and seek salvation. In this Book the plan of salvation is made perfectly clear. All that needs to be known is made known here, so that any man with the Bible in his hand, though his sins are as scarlet, may set himself right with God.

Let it be observed in this connection that Abraham had no Bible. The divine will was communicated to him in dreams and visions and angel visits. He was born a pagan, the son of an idol-maker, and was taught to bow before gods of wood and stone. But the time came when he heard a voice calling him to leave his father's house and go forth into a country that he knew not (Genesis 12:1; Hebrews 11:8), and he followed that voice. He lived up to the full measure of his light, and in that light he read the gospel: *Jesus answered, . . . Abraham rejoiced to see my day: and he saw it, and was glad* (John 8:54, 56). He was thus saved – a pagan born two thousand years before the advent – by faith precisely like ours in the Christ who said, *I am the way, the truth, and the life: no man cometh unto the Father, but by me* (John 14:6).

Notice that the five brothers referred to had the Bible. True, it was only the Old Testament, but that was enough for what was required of them. It contained the Law, and *the man that doeth [the law] shall live in [it]* (Galatians 3:12). But suppose they broke the law. Then they had the gospel in the prophecies, for the prophets all pointed to Christ, who in the fullness of time was to be *wounded for our transgressions, . . . bruised for our iniquities: . . . and with his stripes we [might be] healed* (Isaiah 53:5). The gospel is recorded in the Old Testament as readily as in the New Testament. The tragedy of Calvary runs through it like a scarlet thread. The birth, life, character, vicarious death, and resurrection of Jesus are there so plain that he who runs may read. Therefore the five brothers were without excuse if they did not believe in him.

But how about us? We have the voice of nature, as the heathen have it: *the invisible things of [God] from the creation of the world are clearly seen, being understood by the things that are made, . . . so that [we] are without excuse* (Romans 1:20). We have the voice that speaks from heaven, as Abraham heard it, and if we refuse to hear the voice of the Spirit or fail to live up to this measure of our light, we are again *without excuse*. We have the Old Testament with its messianic prophecies and the New Testament with its evangelists pointing to Christ and showing how all those prophecies were fulfilled in him. Therefore, again and most obviously, we are *without excuse.*

In addition to all this, we have the record of nineteen centuries of Christian progress in which the majestic figure of Christ is seen in the forefront of all the great enterprises of civilization, transforming the home, the workshop, society, and government, ever enlarging and extending the borders of Christendom. What more could we ask? Or how shall we escape if we neglect so great a salvation? Won't the five brothers of the rich man rise up against us in judgment if we sin against our noonday sun? Alas, *this is the condemnation, that light is come into the world, and men loved darkness rather than light* (John 3:19).

Is it to be imagined that if one rose from the dead to admonish us, the result would be different? If Christ himself were to appear at this moment with the glory of the resurrection shining in his face and a troop of archangels following him, would that convince the unconvinced? The chances are they would regard it as a hallucination. The light might dazzle, bewilder, or frighten, but surely it would not remove the unbelief of any who refuse to accept the testimony of the authoritative Word of God.

Chapter 6

Its Literary Value

Some say that the Bible is mere literature and must therefore be subject to the common principles of criticism. For the sake of the argument, let us concede this. Waiving the fact that, unlike all other literature, it is divinely inspired, let us proceed to scrutinize its character as a mere book among books.

And here, as in our last chapter, we shall be helped by a consideration of one of our Lord's parables: namely, the brief parable of the householder and his treasury. It is recorded in Matthew 13:52: *Then he said unto them, Therefore every scribe which is instructed unto the kingdom of heaven is like unto a man that is an householder, which bringeth forth out of his treasure things new and old.*

A traveler is represented here as coming to an oriental home at evening for entertainment. His host, desirous of showing his importance, brings out his treasures and spreads them before him. There were no banks or other places of safe deposit in those days. One's wealth must be buried in the ground or kept in a recess in the wall. The householder goes to his treasury accordingly and brings out things new and old: antique coins, necklaces worn by princes of long ago, golden shields bearing the blows of old-time battles, precious stones plucked from the crowns of captive kings, and the loot of the campaigns of the ages. All these are spread before the eyes of his wondering guest.

Now, says Jesus, the scribe is a custodian of the oracles of God. The key is at his girdle. His business is to bring forth the wealth of Scripture, new truths and old, to dazzle and enchant the beholder's eyes.

A select group of scribes in our time who attribute to themselves the title of "Biblical Experts" will tolerate no trespassing on their prerogative. Over the gateway of the Scriptures, they have placed the caveat:

> N. B. No thoroughfare.
> This preserve is for the use of duly accredited scholars. Ministers and laymen alike are warned off.
> By order of
> The Erudite Junto.

But ministers and laymen are not to be frightened so easily. They insist upon the right of personal judgment in these premises. The words of Jesus, *Search the scriptures,* were not addressed to any pedagogical clique but to the people – all and distinct. The search warrant is in the hands of every man.

To a minister of the gospel, a biblical critic is as an apothecary's apprentice to a physician. The apprentice makes the pills and lotions, knows their constituent parts, and possibly feels himself a master of the *materia medica*. But it will probably be conceded that the physician, whose business is not merely to know what pills and lotions are made of but also how to apply them to the physical life, is somewhat the wiser of the two. Certainly, the young knight of the pestle has his place, but in the practical uses of the pharmacopoeia (drugs), the practicing physician is master of the situation.

So a minister of the gospel, despite the admonition of the Erudite Junto, must insist upon his prerogative in the exposition of the Word. It is his place to know not merely those scriptural infinitesimals, the jots and tittles which men discover with microscopes, but to also know what the Scriptures are good for. It is claimed, therefore, on behalf of ministers of the gospel, that they are quite competent to speak wisely regarding the composition of the Scriptures and their uses.

But when it comes to the literary value of the Scriptures, neither learned professors nor ministers in holy orders can enter any claim superior to that of the average man. These succulent pastures are open alike to all lovers of rhetorical style and beauty.

When Paul, a man of liberal culture, graduate of the University of Jerusalem, was a prisoner at Rome, he wrote to a young friend at Ephesus: *Do thy diligence to come shortly unto me. The cloke that I left at Troas with Carpus, when thou comest, bring with thee, and the books, but especially the parchments* (2 Timothy 4:9, 13). The cloak was for winter days in the Mamertine Prison. The books, probably Greek and oriental treatises, were such as would cheer a scholar's lonely hours. But the parchments, the scrolls of Scripture, were desired above all. *Especially the parchments!* He could, if need be, endure the cold of winter without his cloak; he could get along without the classic poets and philosophers; but the Bible, ah, he must have that, for the treasures of life were in it.

When John Bunyan was a prisoner in Bedford Jail, he found solace for his loneliness in the companionship of books. His library, however, was a very meager one in numbers. His books were only three, but as Mr. Froude significantly says, "One of these was the Bible, which is of itself a liberal education."

In view of the glowing tributes paid by scholars of the centuries to the literary value of the Bible, it is necessary for the devotee of letters to speak with reserve in disparagement of it.

> A glory gilds the sacred page
>   Majestic like the sun;
> It gives a light to every age,
>   It gives but borrows none.
> The Hand that gave it still supplies
>   The gracious light and heat:
> His truths upon the nations rise,
>   They rise but never set.[4]

For the purpose in hand, let us for now erase the name of Jehovah from the title page of the Bible and view it simply as literature, as one of the volumes in the world's library. What other volume is to be compared with it?

I. Its poetry

One-third of the Old Testament is in poetic form. The earliest of its poems, and probably the oldest scrap of poetry in existence, is the "Song of the Sword" in Genesis 4:23-24. It seems to have been commemorative of some primitive feud. A man named Lamech, going out to avenge himself, returns with a song:

> *Adah and Zillah, hear my voice;*
>   *Ye wives of Lamech, hearken unto my speech:*
> *For I have slain a man to my wounding,*
>   *And a young man to my hurt.*
> *If Cain shall be avenged sevenfold,*
>   *Truly Lamech seventy and sevenfold.*

It is scarcely necessary to observe that there is no hint of a divine approval of this bloodthirsty outburst. The record stands without comment, as in many similar cases. It is regrettable that the

---

[4] William Cowper, "The Bible, the Light of the World," 1719.

martial spirit of the "Song of the Sword" has been perpetuated along the succeeding ages.

A most stirring hymn of righteous victory is that of Deborah. "La Marseillaise," "God Save the King," and the "Battle Hymn of the Republic" are flat, stale, and unprofitable beside it. She summons the princes of Israel to the fray. We hear the footfall of the multitude rushing to the high places of the field. The stars in their courses fight against Sisera. The river Kishon, that mighty river, sweeps past in pandemonium, bearing the terror-stricken enemy in utter rout towards the sea. And above the hoarse artillery of heaven, the roar of torrents, and the frightened cries of the vanquished, we hear the song of the prophetess inspiring the victors and invoking revenge upon the cowards of Israel who had lingered among the bleating flocks:

> *O my soul, thou hast trodden down strength.*
> *Curse ye Meroz, said the angel of the* Lord,
> *Curse ye bitterly the inhabitants thereof;*
> *Because they came not to the help of the* Lord,
> *To the help of the* Lord *against the mighty.*
> *The mother of Sisera looked out at a window,*
> *And cried through the lattice,*
> *Why is his chariot so long in coming?*
> *Why tarry the wheels of his chariots?*
> *So let all thine enemies perish, O* Lord.
> (Judges 5:21, 23, 28, 31)

Of this memorable battle song it may be said, as Carlyle wrote of "Scots, wha hae wi' Wallace bled,"[5] that it "should be sung with the voice of the whirlwind."

And where is there anything like Habakkuk's vision from the watchtower? He sees the Almighty marching through history:

---

5   Robert Burns, "Scots Wha Hae," 1793.

> *God came from Teman,*
> *And the Holy One from mount Paran. Selah.*
> *His glory covered the heavens,*
> *And the earth was full of his praise.*
> (Habakkuk 3:3)

Before him goes the pestilence, and burning coals are under his feet; on either side the hills are bowing, and the mountains are scattering. The ocean utters his voice and lifts his crested hands on high. Sun and moon stand still in their habitations at the flash of his speeding arrows and the shining of his spear. With threshing tool in hand, he strides through the centuries, threshing the nations in righteous indignation.

The most familiar, "Hymn of the Springtime," is that of Solomon. All the poets have sung of springtime beauties and the renewal of life, but never one so sweetly as here:

> *My beloved spake, and said unto me,*
> *Rise up, my love, my fair one, and come away.*
> *For, lo, the winter is past,*
> *The rain is over and gone;*
> *The flowers appear on the earth;*
> *The time of the singing of birds is come,*
> *And the voice of the turtle is heard in our land;*
> *The fig tree putteth forth her green figs,*
> *And the vines with the tender grape*
> *Give a good smell.*
> *Arise, my love, my fair one, and come away.*
> (Song of Solomon 2:10-13)

The New Testament opens with the song of the messenger angels: *For unto you is born this day in the city of David a Saviour, which is Christ the Lord. Glory to God in the highest, and on earth peace, good will toward men* (Luke 2:11, 14). Shall we search for anything to equal it? Nowhere shall we find it except in the culminating song of adoration: *Worthy is the Lamb that was slain to receive power, and riches, and wisdom, and strength, and honour, and glory, and blessing* (Revelation 5:12).

These are only a few examples of the inspired poetry which moved John Milton to say, "There are no songs comparable to the songs of Zion." There are other singers like Virgil and Homer, Burning Sappho, Goethe, Schiller, and Shakespeare, but how they dwindle beside the poets of Scripture. They are as twittering swallows in a field of warbling larks. Never have poets sung like those who dipped their pens in "Siloa's brook that flows fast by the oracle of God."[6]

II. Masterpieces of eloquence

We begin with Judah's plea for his brethren at the Egyptian court, probably the oldest example of oratory in existence. He was a shepherd at court, a stranger in a strange land, arraigned with his brothers on a criminal charge. The possibility of death confronted them. The memory of a dreadful secret sin brooded over them. It was under such conditions that Judah presented his argument in their behalf, earnest and pathetic almost unto death. "His fancy," says Dr. Guthrie, "plays with rare delicacy around the respected form of that patriarch, who in the distant home is waiting for Benjamin, and whose very life is bound up in the life of the child." For Benjamin and that aged father, he appeals with tearful fervency: *Now therefore when I come to thy servant my father, and the lad be not with us; . . . it shall come to pass, when he seeth that the lad is not with us, that he will die: and thy servants shall bring down the gray hairs of thy servant our father with sorrow to the grave* (Genesis 44:30-31).

---

6   John Milton, *Paradise Lost,* 1667.

The argument of Moses' plea for the emancipation of Israel is in evidence. Day after day, sixteen times successively, he comes before the tyrant Pharaoh, wielding the rod of Jehovah, and in his name demanding that the chains of his people be broken. How puny the forms of such abolitionists as Wilberforce and Lloyd Garrison seem in the presence of this mighty liberator. *Thus saith the* LORD *God of the Hebrews, Let my people go* (Exodus 9:13). Pharaoh refuses. The river of Egypt rolls red as blood; reptiles infest the land, creeping up even into its kneading troughs; the sun is veiled in darkness; the pestilence stalks abroad; the harvests are beaten down by furious storms of hail; all this until sorrow's crown of sorrow, the lament for the firstborn, rises at midnight from every home. Then the people march forth, three million slaves delivered by the irresistible voice of a single servant of God!

I could tell of Nathan and his parable of the little ewe lamb or of John the Baptist crying in the wilderness: *Repent ye: for the kingdom of heaven is at hand* (Matthew 3:2). Or I could speak of Stephen as he faced death in his eager passion to unveil the frightful sin of the people in crucifying their longed-for Messiah, or of Peter at Pentecost as he preached with such power that three thousand souls are pricked to the heart and fall, sobbing, at the feet of the Savior. Or I could tell of Paul on Mars Hill as he set forth the doctrine of human rights in words that were destined to be a glimpse of all subsequent manifestos concerning civil and ecclesiastical freedom: *[God] hath made of one blood all nations of men for to dwell on all the face of the earth* (Acts 17:26).

But the crowning eloquence of the Scriptures is that of the Master himself. No wonder the common people heard him gladly. *He taught them as one having authority* (Matthew 7:29). They *wondered at the gracious words which proceeded out of his mouth* (Luke 4:22). A Roman guard was sent to arrest him; they paused to listen; they were captivated and returned without their prisoner. *Why have ye not brought him?* demanded their masters. There was never so strange an answer given by men of battle, proof against sentiment, hardened to merciless tasks: *Never man spake like this man* (John 7:45-46).

These are some of the displays of oratory which moved Daniel Webster to say, "If there is aught of power on my lips, it is because of my acquaintance with the eloquence of the Scriptures, which I learned at my mother's knee."

III. Its historical wealth

Here we have the only authentic record of events running back to the infancy of time. All other chronicles are fragmentary. Caesar and Xenophon wrote episodes, but in Scripture are universal chronicles. This deep river flows backward in its course, past the ruined cities of antiquity, in tortuous windings whose roar and thunder are as the confused noise of battle. It flows through the quiet pastures of peace, through the solitudes of primeval ages, and past the confusion of tongues, the deluge, and the creation of man. On it goes past that remote period when the earth was without form and void, onward still beyond the floating nebulae, and even beyond to the indescribable glory where its source is found beneath the heavenly throne, as it is written, *In the beginning God* (Genesis 1:1).

This Book of events has triumphantly passed the ordeal of centuries of adverse criticism. In these last days, the archaeologists, digging among the ruins of ancient cities, have unearthed many confirmations of Holy Writ. Voices have come from mummy crypts, buried forums, and sculptured obelisks, saying with agreement, "Yea" and "Amen" to it.

IV. Scientific propositions of the Bible

It is needless to remind the reader how persistently these have been attacked. It is a common thing to hear it said, "The Bible was not intended to be a scientific book," giving the impression that it makes little difference, therefore, whether its scientific affirmations are correct or not. This, however, is not a matter of negligible significance. If the book is not truthful in this particular area, what ground do we have for committing ourselves to its spiritual guidance? A minister who proves himself unreliable in secular matters, whose word cannot be trusted anywhere except in the pulpit, would not be trusted and pass unchallenged as a spiritual counselor. The question is not whether the Bible was intended to be a scientific book, but whether the Bible is true. It is not true unless it is true and reliable in every way.

The Old Testament Scriptures abound everywhere in scientific statements. They speak of biology, ethnology, astronomy, geology, zoology, and indeed of every department of natural science. You would have to tear the Bible to tatters in order to eliminate such allusions. But neither in general nor in particular have they been successfully impugned. The substantial discoveries of science (observe, I do not say dreams and hypotheses) are continually endorsing and verifying them. It is not to be denied that multitudes of irreligious scientists are vehemently against them. But the Bible, which has withstood the hostile criticism of centuries, is not likely to be affected in this way.

V. Ethics of the Scriptures

By common consent, the Bible is accepted as the standard of universal morals. We take our position between Sinai and Olivet, the two mountains of the law and the gospel, where we find the source of the world's jurisprudence and the sanctions of all civil and social peace and order.

And along with these ethical precepts of Scripture, we find a portrait gallery of worthy men in whom they have been practically illustrated, such as Enoch, Abraham, David, Elijah, Ruth the virtuous, the three Marys, Paul, and the Sons of Thunder. What a roll call of mighty and virtuous persons is found in these inspired pages. Yet all alike are admittedly *concluded all under sin,* and all join in the confession that they *come short of the glory of God* (Galatians 3:22; Romans 3:23).

There is one among them, however, whose face shines as the sun shines in his strength. Over his head we write, "The Wonderful," and under his feet, "*Certainly this was a righteous man*" (Luke 23:47). How it helps struggling men and women to have an ideal so glorious before us. In him we behold the perfect consummation of duty, holiness, manhood, and character. He is the only one who ever lived on earth of whom it could be said, "He was as good as the law." Of him the Nonesuch Professor aptly says, "He brought the bottom of his life up to the top of his light." In him all graces were combined, precisely as all colors blend in the white solar ray – the golden glory of the sunrise, the deep blue of the heavens, and the emerald of the sea. Thus Christ, illustrating in himself all virtues and excellencies, stands forth in history as the ideal Man.

VI. Wealth of doctrine

The Scriptures are of preeminent value in their clear solution to the problems of the spiritual life.

There are some things that all earnest souls are eager to know. We can get along without science, and we can live without the lower forms of knowledge, but we must somehow be informed about the problems of our origin and destiny. Where did we come from and where will we go? Is there a God? Shall we stand before him in judgment? Is there a heaven? Is there a hell? Can a man be delivered from the shame and penalty and power of sin? These are questions that will not diminish. They demand an answer.

All such uncertainties are involved in that old question, "What is truth?" The academy by the river Ilissus, the Painted Porch of Zeno, and the Garden of Epicurus represent vain efforts to answer it. *Canst thou by searching find out God?* (Job 11:7). The despair of the world was expressed by Pilate when he satirically asked, *What is truth?* (John 18:38). But it has pleased God to make known in the Scriptures the things which are beyond our unaided reason.

Other books have poems, but no other sings the song of salvation and gives the troubled soul a peace that flows like a river. Other books have eloquence, but no other enables us to behold God stretching out pierced hands and pleading with men to turn and live. Other books have history, but no other tells the story of divine love reaching from the remote councils of eternity to its consummation on Calvary, "the old, old story of Jesus and his love." Other books have science, but no other can give a man such definite assurance with respect to the future that he can say, *I know whom I have believed, and am persuaded that he is able to keep that which I have committed unto him against that day* (2 Timothy 1:12). Other books set forth philosophy, but no other makes us wise with respect to all those great doctrines which center in the living God.

Let us remember, then, the word of the Master, how he said, *Search the scriptures.* The word is *ereunate*, meaning "to search like a hound on the trail." Search them as for hidden treasure. Blessed, three times blessed, is the man who, by such searching, finds the secret of eternal life.

> This is the field where hidden lies
> The pearl of price unknown;
> The merchant is divinely wise
> Who makes that pearl his own.[7]

In our childhood we were led by imagination into subterranean caves, where vaulted roofs and chafed walls sparkled with precious stones. Thus, to the reader whose eyes are opened by the touch of the Spirit, the Scriptures glow with the unspeakable riches of truth. But amongst their countless splendors, there is none so wonderful as Christ himself. He is the *Kohinoor*, the crown jewel of them all.

These are the literary marvels of the Bible; is it in any way surprising that it should be the best seller in the book markets of the world today?

---

7   Isaac Watts, "The Excellence of Scripture," 1709.

Chapter 7

Its Up-to-Dateness

The Bible is the oldest book in the world. A considerable part of it was old enough to be out of date, had it not been immune against the ravages of time, when Cecrops founded Egypt. We speak of Chaucer as the father of Anglo-Saxon literature, but the book of Job was current three thousand years before Dan Chaucer opened the "well of English undefiled."[8] Dr. Johnson read the sweet drama of Ruth aloud in a literary club at a time when infidelity was widespread; great was the amazement of his listeners when, in answer to their exclamation, "Where did you find it?" he answered, "This was written twenty-five hundred years before Columbus was born!"

Yet, strange to say, this oldest of books is the freshest of all. No other will bear reading over and over with "new light ever bursting from it." Dr. Elliot, sitting by the window with a Bible on his knees, when asked by his daughter what he was reading, replied, "The news, my dear, always the good news!"

The poet Goethe said, "The Bible becomes more and more beautiful the more I study it." There are millions of people who are searching the Scriptures year in and year out and finding

---

8   *Dan* is an archaic title equivalent to *Master* or *Sir*.

them as fresh as the break of day. This is because the Bible was so constructed by divine wisdom to anticipate progress. Its truths, its ethical precepts, and its exceedingly great and precious promises are like oriental spices which, the more they are rubbed, give forth more of the fragrant sweetness. The gospel is indeed the last tidings from the heaven of a loving God.

There are men posing as liberal and progressive who speak patronizingly of the Bible as a "back number" (earlier issue of a magazine), good enough perhaps for its time but far behind the days we are living in. The trouble with them, however, is that they have failed to keep abreast of progress. They are like the Danites who, defaulting in loyalty to the ark of the covenant and its Book of the Law, were condemned to *go hindmost with their standards* (Numbers 2:31).

There have always been Danites in the church: self-sufficient, arrogant, heedless of authority, and disloyal to the Book of the Law. In our time they call themselves liberal because of their liberalism toward all but loyalists and progressives, despite their rejection of the Scriptures which are always in the forefront. In fact, they are behind the times, and despite their clamorous insistence on leadership, they do go *hindmost [last] with their standards* in the procession of events.

They say they love the Bible, but their devotion to it is like that of Abner for Asahel who, while greeting him affectionately, was fumbling for his dagger that he might *smite him under the fifth rib* (2 Samuel 2:23). They profess loyalty to the church, but like a serpent by the way, they *biteth the heels* of the Lord's cavalry as it pursues its evangelistic march forward. They profess a profound reverence for Christ, but they insist that those who follow his teaching and example in the defense of the Scriptures are far behind the age. Are they right? If so, Christ and his apostles, and the ministry in general, and the great body of believers in the universal church throughout the world are desperately wrong in following the ark of the covenant with its Book of the Law.

1. All loyalists maintain that the Bible, as a book of science, is ahead of the age.
As we open the Bible, we immediately come to these words: *In the beginning God created the heaven and the earth* (Genesis 1:1). Here are three scientific propositions in a row, all dealing with the origin of things.

To begin with, we have *God:* not law, nor energy, nor a headless, heartless, heedless soul of the universe. We have one to whom we can lift our eyes and say, *Our Father,* a Father with eyes to see, a heart to pity, and an arm to protect, *when the blast of the terrible ones is as a storm against the wall* (Isaiah 25:4).

Then God *created.* This scientific proposition is presented with three counter propositions: namely, the eternity of matter, autogenesis, and evolution. The first of these is a grotesque attempt to cut the Gordian Knot.[9] The second is a dogma without a trace of evidence, since nobody is able to exhibit so much as one self-producing midget or grain of sand. And the third is a pure hypothesis, which many of the leading scientists have abandoned on the ground that it does not afford a working theory of origins.

Still further, God created the heavens and the earth and all things therein in a definite order. And the order of creation as laid down is confirmed by leading cosmologists. It is a singular fact that a book written so many thousands of years ago should have anticipated the researches of the later centuries. How shall we account for it? There was a time when those who called themselves advanced thinkers insisted that there was a mistake in the Genesis statement as to the existence of light before the sun, but nobody says so now; everybody knows that

---

9   The term *Gordian Knot* is used to describe a complex or unsolvable problem, traced to a legendary time in the life of Alexander the Great.

frictional or electric light must have existed in the confusion of chaos before the appearance of the sun. Therefore, the scientific propositions of the Scriptures called into question one by one have survived criticism and have emerged as proven facts.

So if any of us are posing as progressives, it would be well to take heed or we may be found *hindmost in the ranks*. Let us put our ears to the ground and listen to things that are going on.

2. Now let us consider the Bible as a book of history.
It is worth noting that those who call themselves liberals, progressives, higher critics, and advanced thinkers insist that the Scriptures were really intended to show historically the evolution of a nation, and in the same breath affirm that their historicity is not to be depended on. But all attempts to cast reproach on their historical truthfulness are utterly vain. *There is a generation, O how lofty are their eyes! and their eyelids are lifted up* (Proverbs 30:13).

The Pentateuch, made up of the five books of Moses, has naturally been the center of attack. It has been stigmatized as a collection of myths and fables and folklore, little better than the preposterous *Tales of Baron Munchausen*. There are theological professors who frankly hold that view.

It was not long ago that certain progressives were hesitant to affirm boldly that there never was any such person as Moses, because no mention of him could be found in other records. And, allowing that there was such a man, they believed that he couldn't possibly have written the Pentateuch, because the art of writing was unknown in his time. Then along came a man with a spade, and digging among the ruins of Tell el-Amarna, he unearthed a whole library of correspondence carried on by the kings of Babylon before Moses was even born.

They said that Exodus was a myth, for how could there have been such an insurrection of millions of slaves without some mention of it in contemporary records? Then along came the man with the spade who began digging in the valley of the Nile. Presently he came upon a burial crypt with a mummy of the pharaoh of the exodus, wrapped in byssus bands on which was inscribed the departure of the fugitives.

But, in any case, it was insisted that there were no Hittites; no such formidable nation as the Israelites are said to have encountered them in the subjugation of Canaan, for surely a nation that important would have been mentioned somewhere else. The man with the spade appeared again, and in the valley of the Euphrates he unearthed seals and cylinders and ruined cities which certified not only the fact that the Hittites existed, but also that they conquered Egypt and flourished at the very time indicated in the Pentateuch as the greatest of the great powers of those days.

Let the Danites take heed and beware of men with spades. For it has pleased the God of the Scriptures to leave a trial ledger in the deep places of the earth, by which the arrogant claims of those who deny the historical authenticity of the inspired records may at any moment be put to an open shame.

3. Now let us return to the Bible as a masterpiece of literature.
It is, as I have repeatedly said, the oldest book in the world. How shall we account for its existence today? Old books die. Where are *Novum Organum, Hydriotaphia,* and *Eikonoklastes*? You do not even recognize their names? Yet these were the three epoch-making books of their time. *Novum Organum,* by Lord Bacon, introduced with new emphasis the inductive system of philosophy. *Hydriotaphia,* by Sir Thomas Browne, was regarded as the most comprehensive thesaurus of knowledge produced thus far. And *Eikonoklastes,* by John Milton, was the monumental defense of popular rights as against the divine right of

kings. Where are they now? Yet the old Bible still lives and is the best seller in the book markets of the world.

But if the Bible has such surpassing merit from the literary point of view, why should there be such a prejudice against it? Can it be that our progressive friends have been so busily engaged in studying its outside that they are actually ignorant of its contents? Such things have been known.

There never was a more progressive body of men than the free-thinking members of the Encyclopédie in France a hundred years ago, but when Benjamin Franklin read to them a chapter of Scripture beginning with *God came from Teman, and the Holy One from mount Paran* (Habakkuk 3:3), they exclaimed with one accord, "Wonderful! Wonderful! But who wrote it?"

When he replied, "This is the prayer of Habakkuk," they cried, "Habakkook! Who is Habakkook? We never heard of him."

It is common now that young men are going out of some of our theological seminaries armed with all sorts of information against the authenticity of the Bible, but when examined, they prove to be hopelessly ignorant of what is recorded in it.

4. Finally, consider the Bible as a religious book.
And here is the real secret of the opposition to the Bible: *The carnal mind is enmity against God* (Romans 8:7), and the moment you open the Bible, you come upon some tremendous truths that center in him.

The first of these is God himself, whom the Athenian mind explains away that no altar is left except one inscribed TO THE UNKNOWN GOD (Acts 17:23).

The second truth is man, made in God's likeness but lost in sin; his birthright is gone and *Ichabod* is written on his forehead: *The glory is departed* (1 Samuel 4:21). This is attributed to an incident known as "the fall." But the fall is denied. Forty years ago one of our leading liberals said, "If man ever fell, he fell up." He would scarcely say so today, however, because the last forty years have witnessed the formulation and general acceptance of a scientific doctrine known as heredity, which is almost literally a paraphrase of original sin.

The third of the religious truths of Scripture is the reconciliation of sinful man with a holy God. Here emerges the cross. *God so loved the world, that he gave his only begotten Son, that whosoever believeth in him should not perish, but have everlasting life* (John 3:16). As the vicarious atonement is practically denied by all so-called progressives, it surely gives way to show them how the wayward child and the offended Father can be brought into an *at-one-ment* (togetherness or reconciliation) in some other way. But the Bible way is the only way. "The Jesus road," as the Apaches call it, is the only road back to God. There is no suggestion in the Qur'an or any other of the sacred books, or in science or philosophy, or anywhere else of any other plan for blotting out the sinful past. It is only the blood of Jesus Christ that cleanses from sin.

These doctrines find the most strenuous objection, but these very doctrines are abreast of current thought. The arguments against them are so old that I marvel at the foolhardiness of the man who reproduces them. Celsus Redivivus, Porphyry, Julian the Apostate, Spinoza, Diderot, Jean-Jaques Rousseau, Voltaire, Thomas Paine, Strauss, Ernest Renan, and Theodore Parker – behold them parading in many of our pulpits and professors' chairs. Up to date, in truth? Not among such Danites, bringing up the rear of the procession, will you hear the bugle call of progress in these days.

In one of the battles of our Civil War, a regiment was commanded to charge upon a Confederate battery, which they proceeded to do. But meeting with unexpected opposition, they were ordered to retreat. The color-bearer, however, not hearing the order, marched straight on. "Bring back that flag!" called the colonel.

"Bring up your men!" replied the color-bearer. The ark of the covenant hears no order to retreat. The Book of the Law "floateth like a banner" in the vanguard of Israel.[10] It waits not for Danites who abide at home. "The royal standards onward go!"[11]

The Bible has come to stay. The old challenge of Isaiah holds good: *The voice said, Cry. And he said, What shall I cry? All flesh is grass, and all the goodliness thereof is as the flower of the field: the grass withereth, the flower fadeth: because the spirit of the* Lord *bloweth upon it: surely the people is grass. The grass withereth, the flower fadeth: but the word of our God shall stand for ever* (Isaiah 40:6-8).

Thus it is written and thus it must be, for the mouth of the Lord has spoken it.

---

10 William Walsham How, "O Word of God Incarnate," 1867.
11 Venantius Honorius Clementianus Fortunatus, "The Royal Standard Forward Goes," 569.

Chapter 8

Its Tone of Authority

There are three lines of evidence in favor of Christianity: namely, oral testimony, Scripture, and personal experience. When combined, these are conclusive and irrefutable. *A threefold cord is not quickly broken* (Ecclesiastes 4:12).

First: Oral Testimony
Peter says, *We have not followed cunningly devised fables, when we made known unto you the power and coming of our Lord Jesus Christ, but were eyewitnesses of his majesty. For he received from God the Father honour and glory, when there came such a voice to him from the excellent glory, This is my beloved Son, in whom I am well pleased. And this voice which came from heaven we heard, when we were with him in the holy mount* (2 Peter 1:16-18).

The apostle was speaking to those who had not seen Jesus in the flesh. He himself had heard his sermons, seen his miracles, and witnessed his wonderful life. In particular, he had been with him on the Mount of Transfiguration, had seen his homespun garments flutter aside for a moment revealing the royal purple, and had heard the voice saying, *This is my beloved*

Son. All this was no dream, no fable, and no hallucination; he had seen and heard it. And others who were eyewitnesses were prepared to testify in like manner as to the divine character and mission of Christ. This sort of testimony is still offered to sustain the gospel claim.

But you say, "This is mere hearsay." We answer:

(1) Such hearsay has valid weight as evidence. In fact, we continually accept evidence of this sort without a murmur. How do we know that light travels at the rate of 186,000 miles per second? Only because certain persons, after investigation, have said so. How do we know that sad remnants of the British and German fleets are lying at the bottom of the North Sea? Men who were present have told us so. How do we know that Croton water is fit to drink? We rest on the assurance of scientists who have analyzed it. I suppose that 99 percent of our knowledge comes by hearsay. We receive the testimony of eyewitnesses as a matter of course unless there is some definite reason for rejecting it.

(2) Such evidence, in favor of Christianity, has a cumulative value for us. In Peter's time, there were only a few witnesses who could say, *That which was from the beginning, which we have heard, which we have seen with our eyes, which we have looked upon, and our hands have handled, of the Word of life; . . . declare we unto you* (1 John 1:1, 3). We, on the contrary, have the testimony of a great multitude which no man can number. For the little procession of eleven men who originally came down the outer stairway from an upper room in Jerusalem has increased through the centuries from hundreds to thousands, and from thousands to hundreds of millions. They have passed by the light of burning at the stake and under the shadow of dungeons and gallows, declaring the testimony of Jesus and

singing his praise in hosannas that blend like a chorus of many waters and mighty thunderings that issue from the heavenly gates. Hundreds of millions of Christians living today are prepared to testify of their personal experience in the truth of the Scriptures. They certify with one accord: "We were sinners, troubled with a certain fearful anticipation of judgment. We came to the written Word for knowledge as to the incarnate Word, and upon finding Christ, we have found salvation through faith in him. Thus the peace that *passeth all understanding* has come into our hearts. *We have not followed cunningly devised fables.* We speak from experience. *[We] know whom [we] have believed, and [are] persuaded that he is able to keep that which [we] have committed unto him against that day.*

It is submitted that so great a body of testimony is of overwhelming weight. To a reasonable man, it must be quite conclusive, unless some definite rebuttal is brought forth. Certainly no court of justice would reject it.

Second: Scripture Itself
Of this Peter goes on to say, *We have also a more sure word of prophecy* [more sure than hearsay]; *whereunto ye do well that ye take heed, as unto a light that shineth in a dark place, until the day dawn, and the day star arise in your hearts: knowing this first, that no prophecy of the scripture is of any private interpretation. For the prophecy came not in old time by the will of man: but holy men of God spake as they were moved by the Holy Spirit* (2 Peter 1:19-21).

The fact that Scripture is *more sure* than oral testimony is clearly based upon its ultimate authority as the inspired and true Word of God.

It is obvious that somewhere there must be a final criterion of truth. There are standards of weight and measure in Washington for the testing of every pound and yardstick in our country. It cannot be assumed that the heavenly Father would set his children adrift without a trustworthy chart for their direction. This is the rationale of the Scriptures. They were intended to be an ultimate and infallible rule of faith and conduct. And they are so received, despite all controversy by the universal church. The man who rejects them is bound in justice to himself to discover some other court of final authority where he may seek a confirmation of spiritual things amidst the noise of conflicting voices.

The apostle justifies his confidence in the Scriptures by adding that they *came not . . . by the will of man: but holy men of God spake as they were moved by the Holy Spirit.* If this means anything, it means that the men who wrote the Scriptures did not sit down by themselves with stylus and parchment, saying, "I will write an account of the creation," or, "I will write the history of Israel," or, "I will write a prediction of the Messiah," or, "I will write doctrine and ethics." They proceeded to their work and performed it under the immediate direction and control of the Spirit of God. The figure is that of a vessel under sail. They were *moved* by the divine breath as a ship is borne onward by the wind filling its canvas. In other words, they wrote what they were directed to write by the Spirit of God.

Still further, the apostle says that the Scriptures so written are not *of any private interpretation.* The word here rendered *private* is *idia,* literally "one's own." This means that no man is his own interpreter. When we speak of the right of private judgment with reference to Scripture, we mean to exclude all human intervention between the soul and God, but too bad for one who approaches revelation in the dim light of his own unaided reason. The finite cannot grasp the infinite. Spiritual things are *spiritually discerned* (1 Corinthians 2:14). God, who gave the Scriptures, must help us to understand them. Therefore, the Holy Spirit, by whom the sacred page is illuminated, is represented as *anoint[ing our] eyes with eyesalve*, that we may wisely read it (Revelation 3:18).

The chancellor of Queen Candace, riding in his chariot with the sacred scroll of the prophet Isaiah before him, knit his brows in perplexity as he read the messianic prediction: *He is brought as a lamb to the slaughter, and as a sheep before her shearers is dumb, so he openeth not his mouth* (Isaiah 53:7). Philip, the evangelist, walking alongside and hearing him, asked, *Understandest thou what thou readest? And he said, How can I, except some man should guide me?* He was then guided by Philip, and immediately the truth flashed upon him (Acts 8:30-31).

Third: Personal Experience

We are like wanderers in the night; voices are heard around us, saying, "*This is the way, walk ye in it.*" Better still, the Bible is given to us as a lantern *that shineth in a dark place,* but when we see the light of the morning, our perplexity is over (2 Peter 1:19). Thus, personal experience adds final confirmation to oral testimony and Scripture. Peter says we do well to listen to the word of eyewitnesses and to give heed to the lamplight of prophecy *until the day dawn, and the day star arise in [our] hearts* (2 Peter 1:19).

A woman once came running into the city of Samaria, saying, "I went out to Jacob's well to draw water, and a wayfarer met me who spoke as never a man spoke of spiritual things; he *told me all things that ever I did.* Is not this the Messiah for whom we have been looking? Come and see" (John 4:29). Her friends and neighbors followed her back to the well and heard him. They asked him to be their guest, and he stayed with them two days; many believed because of his word. Then they said to the woman, *Now we believe, not because of thy saying: for we have heard him ourselves, and know that this is indeed the Christ, the Saviour of the world* (John 4:42). Thus, in the end a man is convinced and saved only by personal experience when he can say, "I have met Christ, have made his acquaintance, have reasoned with him by the way, and have learned to reverence and love him."

It is evident, however, that the final reference with respect to spiritual truth is to the Bible itself. Hearsay is not infallible; personal experience is confined to the limits of a single soul, but the Scriptures are the court of final appeal because they speak with the authority of a supreme and omniscient God.

It might be assumed that a book like this, dealing with spiritual truths all of which lie beyond the scope of the physical senses, would speak with some measure of reserve or uncertainty, but there are no ifs or perhapses here. How could a divine book speak that way? We want no guesses about life and immortality. We must know. We want authority, and there can be no final authority with respect to such problems except that of a divine *ipse dixit* (assertion). Therefore, the Bible always says, *Yea, and . . . Amen;* and *Thus saith the* LORD; and *Verily, verily, I say unto you.*

Put an *if* into the Ten Commandments and you lay a charge of dynamite under the morality of men and nations. Put an *if* under the manger at Bethlehem, and you destroy the happiness of a million homes. Put an *if* under Calvary, and you make Christians the most miserable of all men. Put an *if* under the empty sepulcher in Joseph's garden, and immediately our visions of life and immortality vanish into thin air. But blessed be God, there are no ifs in the Bible. It gives no uncertain sound. It speaks as becomes the oracles of God.

Chapter 9

Its Trustworthiness

No claim of inerrancy is made for the King James Version of the Scriptures, nor for any other of the multitudinous versions current in the world today.

It is claimed first, however, that the original manuscripts, as they left the hands of *holy men of God [who wrote] as they were moved by the Holy Spirit,* must have been free from error in the fundamentals of the case (2 Peter 1:21). Second, the errors in existing copies are of such a character as to convince an unprejudiced mind that the originals were without a flaw.

Whether the assurance of such inerrancy in the original writing is worthwhile is another question. There are those who say, "What does it matter whether the writings on sheepskin scrolls which perished long centuries ago were flawless or not? We never saw them and have practically nothing to do with them."[12]

To these we answer: First, our belief in their integrity has a vital bearing not only on our opinion of the truthfulness of God, but also on the character of those who claimed to be moved by his Spirit in declaring his holy will. It is possible to conceive that

---

12 Since the writing of this book, many ancient scrolls or partial scrolls have been found and seen.

a man whose mother died before he set eyes upon her might be wholly indifferent to the question of whether she was a good woman or not, but most of us would feel differently about it.

Our second answer to the man who criticizes the importance of believing in the integrity of the original writings is that our view with respect to that matter cannot help but influence our attitude toward the trustworthiness of current versions. A thirsty traveler will readily drink from a brook by the wayside if he can trace its flow back to a clear fountain in the high hills. He knows that the slight impurities due to the wearing down of its banks have not impaired its wholesomeness. If, on the other hand, he were uncertain as to whether its origin were in a spring or a cesspool, he would hesitate until he found out.

Our third answer to the critics is that the discrepancies in current versions are of such a character as to furnish presumptive proof of the entire correctness of the originals. It would naturally be supposed that a book of such antiquity and of such complex composition would suffer all sorts of disastrous changes in coming down through the ages. Think of the tens of thousands of hands through which it has passed – the copies made by the ancient scribes with infinite pains, the numberless transcriptions by medieval monks in their lonely cells, and the translations into half a thousand languages and dialects. What possibilities for error! Remember, all these transcribers and translators were fallible men. Think of the temptation on their part to interject their personal views into the body of the inspired text or to eliminate what did not please them. Think of what sort of Bible we would have if these transcribers and translators had been like the higher critics of our time, such as those so-called biblical experts who, striving like the mountain in the proverb, brought forth that grotesquerie known as the Polychrome Bible. Think of these possibilities, and then look at the Scriptures as they are in the current versions of today.

The marvel is not that there are variations and discrepancies here, but that they are so trivial and insignificant. They are indeed of such a character as to convince any candid mind that they had no place in the original writing but have crept into the text in the process of transmission through the ages.

Important to note, none of these variations affect the integrity of the doctrine and ethics of the Bible to the slightest degree. If the destructive critics are taken at their word, the Bible is full of frightful errors. Its prophecies have failed; its history is unhistorical; its science is unscientific, and its chronicles are myths. Scarcely does it need to be said that as far as being a true statement of the case, not a single error has yet been indicated which cannot be most reasonably explained as either purely imaginary or unimportant. But here is a marvelous thing: these enemies of Scripture are themselves insistent with one another that the errors in the Bible which they so loudly exploit do not in any degree impair the integrity of its doctrinal system and ethical code.

These things being so, we have reason to conclude that the inspired Bible has in some manner been singularly safeguarded in its passage through the centuries. The same gracious God who protected his secretaries – those *holy men of God [who wrote] as they were moved by the Holy Spirit* – from all possibility of error in the original writing, has apparently by a special providence so protected the flying scroll in its journey down to us. He did this in such a way that transcribers and translators have left an infallible rule of faith and practice in the versions now current among men.

If it be urged again that we are not practically concerned with the original writing, inasmuch as no living man has ever seen it, we observe that an equal objection could be offered against Christ himself with equal force on precisely the same grounds. The objection proves either too little or too much. No living man has ever seen the incarnate Word of God. He lived only thirty-three years in this world of ours and then vanished from sight. The only knowledge that we have of him, apart from the Scriptures, is through his followers, for every Christian is, so to speak, a current version of the incarnate Word. Christ, like the Bible, has suffered by transcription through the ages.

It is nevertheless of supreme importance that we should believe that Christ, as he once lived on earth, was the perfect Son of God. The very mistakes of believers in their earnest yet inadequate efforts to copy his life and character are evidences of his perfection. We are always striving to get back to the original Christ – precisely as reverent students of the Scriptures seek, by both textual and historical criticism, to reach the original text – that is, the first edition of the written Word of God.

Chapter 10

Its Influence on Personal Life

The ultimate test of life and character was appropriately set forth by our Lord and Savior in the words, *Ye shall know them by their fruits*. And the question that followed was one that appealed to the common sense of all: *Do men gather grapes of thorns, or figs of thistles?* (Matthew 7:16).

Certainly not. If a man wants a cluster of grapes, he will go to a vineyard for it and not to a thicket of thorns. Or if he is searching for figs, he will not go to Scotland, "the land of the thistle," but to Arabia, "the garden of figs."

Why? Because like produces like. This is one of nature's laws. *And God said, Let the earth bring forth grass, the herb yielding seed, and the fruit tree yielding fruit after his kind, whose seed is in itself, upon the earth: and it was so* (Genesis 1:11).

Here is the criterion by which we determine the difference between brambles and berry bushes, between the false and the true. The law works without exception in every department of human life and observation, and it furnishes a standard of judgment by which to test infallibly the moral quality of things.

Suppose now the Bible is judged in that way.

There are millions of books in circulation. At a table generously furnished, the judicious reader will not eat at random but will pick and choose, selecting what is best for him. The test question is, "What is the fruit of this or that book?" Does it lighten life's burdens with innocent laughter? Does it inform the mind? Does it clarify the conscience? Does it strengthen the will that makes for a noble life? Will it enable me to contribute to the betterment of the world I am living in? And does it furnish the right sort of preparation for the life further on?

It has been customary lately to publish *The World's Greatest Books,* volumes with lists of those books which have most deeply and broadly influenced life and character. Everyone might agree on Chaucer's *The Canterbury Tales,* Raleigh's *The History of the World,* Sir Thomas More's *Utopia,* Locke's *An Essay Concerning Human Understanding,* Bunyan's *The Pilgrim's Progress,* Newton's *Principia,* Walton's *The Compleat Angler,* Sir Thomas Browne's *Hydriotaphia,* Milton's *Paradise Lost,* Butler's *The Analogy of Religion,* Boswell's *The Life of Samuel Johnson,* unknown author's *The Letters of Junius,* Spenser's *The Faerie Queen,* and Gibbon's *Decline and Fall of the Roman Empire;* but there is a wide difference of opinion concerning even these.

Here, however, is a singular fact: no matter how many such lists are prepared or who prepares them, you will invariably find them including one book – namely, the Bible. This fact is worth emphasizing, because it indicates a practical consensus of opinion that this particular Book is likely to do good, inasmuch as it has been doing good and only good all the days of its life thus far.

It is frequently said of the Bible that in order to arrive at a fair judgment respecting its merits, we must criticize it like other books. For the sake of the argument again, so be it. Here is the criterion: "By its fruits ye shall know it."

And fortunately, its fruits are known. History furnishes abundant data for a comparison of its influence with that of other books. The fact that it exists at all is an illustration of the survival of the fittest, and therefore a tribute to its excellence. The reason it survives is that it is the one book which the world and the centuries, familiar with its power, would not willingly let die.

What is its influence on individual character? In other words, what sort of men and women does it make? Call the roll of the mighties: the noble army of martyrs, pioneers of truth, philanthropists, public benefactors like Howard and Wilberforce, philosophers like Locke and Bacon, scientists like Newton and Faraday, reformers like Luther and Knox, missionaries like Xavier and Livingstone, statesmen like William the Silent and Washington and Lincoln, poets like Milton, historians like Guizot, and scholars like the learned Grotius. The time would fail me to tell of those who, drawing their inspiration from this Book, have written their names in the memory and gratitude of men.

But we, being humble folk, are more concerned with the fruit of the Bible as tested in the life and character of the average man. How about your own father and mother, who loved the Bible and adjusted their lives to it? Or how about your friends and neighbors who profess to believe and practice it? Do they seem to be helped or hurt by their devotion to its precepts? Did you ever hear of a man or woman who was demoralized by it? Are there any better people in the world than those who consistently live by it? Do you know of anybody who ever plucked apples of Sodom from the branches of this tree?

"By its fruits ye shall know it."

Suppose we apply this criterion of judgment to other "sacred books."

If you desire to know the influence of *The Analects of Confucius,* look at the Chinese. One who has lived in that country for many years says, "There is no mode of deception or fraud in which these people are not adept. Lying is so common that they have almost lost the consciousness that it is wrong. Quarreling, slandering and cursing, intrigues and brawls are universal. Theft, extortion, robbery, piracy, suicide, infanticide, murder, lotteries, gambling shops, and opium dens are common everywhere." How could it be otherwise when Confucianism, distinctly a moral and not a religious system, admittedly makes no recognition of God?

If you wish to know the fruits of the Vedas (Hindu scriptures), look at the Brahmans of India, among whom there is an open, shameless, and prevalent disregard of practically all the deep-founded and eternal distinctions between right and wrong. Abbe Dubois[13] says, "I have never seen a religious procession in India without its presenting to me the image of hell." The holiest of Brahmans is the twice-born yogi, who sits by the roadside naked, with hair uncombed, and the Vedas before him. His body is smeared with ashes and dung. Ask him what he is doing, and he will tell you he is "losing himself in the ineffable One." His mystical sentence is "I am God! I am God!" He lives uselessly and dies obstinately with that blasphemy on his lips.

If you want to know the fruits of the Tripitaka,[14] behold them exemplified in the life and character of the Buddhists. The central thought of their philosophy is expressed in the term *Nirvana,* which means the ultimate extinction of personality, as the perfume of the lotus flower is exhaled in air or as a drop of water sinks into the sea. They thus profess to believe in immortality, but who cares to be immortal when he does not know it? The result is apparent, says a writer: "In the cities of the dead, where tens of thousands lie unburied waiting for a lucky day; in the ringing of gongs and discharging of fireworks

---

13   Abbe J.A. Dubois (January 1765—February 17, 1848) was a French Catholic missionary in India.
14   *Tripitaka* means "Triple Basket," which is the traditional term for ancient collections of Buddhist sacred scriptures.

to keep away the evil spirits; in the incantations over the sick and honors paid to dead beggars to appease their ghosts; and in the pampering of monkeys and sacred pigs, as a work of merit, while men and women die of starvation in the streets."

Do you know the character of the Qur'an? Read it in the light of the recent massacres in Turkey. The three outstanding facts of Islam are war, slavery, and sensuality – the sword, the auction block, and the harem! What would you expect to pluck from Muhammad's tree? Its legitimate fruit is barbarism. Its mosques are planted in the regions of darkness and the shadow of death.

Now, would you desire to know the Bible? Test it under the same law of fruit-bearing.

It proposes to save men from the penalty and power of sin. Of all the religions in the world, this is the only one that suggests the possibility of blotting out a sinful past and thereby removing the handicap to hope and aspiration.

It proposes also to sanctify the forgiven sinner or, in other words, to build up his character in truth and righteousness. And it does this by placing him under the transforming power of the Spirit of God.

Thus, the Bible develops character. Who shall explain the subtle metaphysical force in this Book which somehow gets hold of the lingering possibilities in the soul of a reprobate and transforms him and changes his heart, conscience, and will, thus making a new man of him?

Has any other book such power? Does the Qur'an or the Zend-Avesta[15] transform men in this manner and set their faces toward righteousness and heaven and God? An old Highlander once said to Claudius Buchanan, "I cannot argue with you; I cannot present theological facts or reasons; I cannot explain the philosophy of revelation; but I know this, that when I was a

---

15 The Zend-Avesta is the sacred book of Zoroastrianism.

man of evil character, the Bible got hold of me and quelled the tiger in me!" There is the master fact: This Book makes men. The best people – here, there, everywhere, and always – are those who believe in the Bible and live that way.

If this fact is questioned, let us put it to a practical test. Take the *Charities Directory of the City of New York*. This is a compendium of more than ten thousand organized forms of charity, and the singular fact is that these contributions are practically all carried out by friends of the Bible. The exceptions are so few that they can be enumerated on the fingers of a dozen men.

The critics of the Bible and of religious people profess to be doing wonders for the regeneration of society, but they are doing nothing of the sort. Words, words, loud boastful words! *By their fruits ye shall know them.*

Not that the friends of the Bible are above criticism. On the contrary, they are vulnerable at many points, and nobody knows it better than themselves. They do not claim to be good people but are only trying to be good and finding it no easy task. The really "good" people are all outside pointing their fingers at them. And meanwhile these derided folk are serving the world fairly well.

This is a point to be emphasized in view of the frequent rebukes which are passed on religious people for their alleged indifference to the demands of social service. It is not an uncommon thing to hear outsiders say, "You churchmen and Bible folk are so devoted to otherworldliness that you care little or nothing for the sufferings of people here and now. While you are sending Bibles to Borrioboola-Gha, the needy are clamoring all around you. Why don't you feed the hungry and clothe the naked and do something to make this world a better place to live in?"

It would naturally be supposed that people who talk that way would themselves be very busily engaged in advancing the temporal welfare of their fellow men, but statistics and observation do not point that way. There are, it is true, individual cases of philanthropy among the non-religious, but the exceptions are relatively so few and individually so conspicuous as merely to prove the rule referred to.

Christian philanthropy, however, is differentiated from secular philanthropy by the fact that it does not concern itself exclusively with the temporal welfare of men. It does not confine itself to that small arc of the great circle which is called time, but deals with man as an immortal being. It reasons like this: "While it falls on me to smooth the earthly pathway of man as far as possible, my supreme effort must always be devoted to his preparation for the unending eons of existence that await him. Therefore, while I minister to his physical needs, I must never forget the demands of his immortal soul." This is the philosophy of "a loaf of bread wrapped in a tract." This is why the call "Come to Jesus" can never lose its timeliness. One who accepts the teaching of the Scriptures must believe that eternity is longer than time and formulate his life accordingly. Therefore, the reproach of "otherworldliness" is not well taken. The best man is the man who lives with eternity in view and that not only for himself but also for the next man. And this is the sort of man that the Bible makes – a far-seeing, right-living, man-loving man.

The friends of the Bible are usually the best people in the world. If that statement is challenged, let us test it. Take a hundred people at random from among those who profess to believe in the Bible and strive to conform their lives to it; then take another hundred at random from those who reject the teachings of the Bible. Place them in opposite lines for comparison. We will cheerfully await the results.

On the one hand, among the unbelievers, you will certainly find many who are notoriously wrong livers. Horace Greeley once remarked that while all the members of the opposing political party were not horse-thieves, he was prepared to say that all horse-thieves belonged to that party. In like manner, while it is not claimed that all those who hate the Bible are conspicuously disreputable, it goes without saying that all notorious reprobates of every sort – rogues, rum-sellers, corrupt agitators, enemies of society and government – are opposed to the Scriptures.

On the other hand, your hundred true lovers of the Bible stand solidly for everything that makes for a square deal in this present world, for the uplifting of the community, defense of law and order, and for the betterment of men not only here but also hereafter. It is alleged that there are hypocrites among them. But why should attention be called to this fact? Do we ever hear of phony atheists or infidels? Why not? Because imitation in such cases would not be worthwhile. Men do not counterfeit leather medals, but they do fake golden eagles.

And why, when a Christian falls from grace, should he be ridiculed for it? The fingers of the people are pointed at him. The newspapers blazon his guilt in such headlines as "Another Deacon Gone Wrong." Are atheists, infidels, and Bible-haters treated in that manner? If one of them offends against morality, is he derided for it? Do the newspapers ever announce "Another Infidel Entangled with the Law"? Why not? Because the world recognizes the logical fitness of things. It knows that when a man without religious principle offends against the foundations of truth and righteousness, he only does what is expected of him. But when a Christian is inconsistent, he offends not only against Christ but also against public opinion, since everybody knows what a Christian ought to be.

We do not undertake to explain the metaphysical force in the Bible – the force that is likened to a *twoedged sword, piercing even to the dividing asunder of soul and spirit* of a man – but conversion is a fact, an indisputable fact. The chancellor of Queen Candace was converted by reading the fifty-third chapter of Isaiah, and centuries later Lord Rochester, a virulent infidel, was converted by reading the same. This sort of thing is going on all the time. Has any other book such power? Do the Shastra, the Zend-Avesta, the Qur'an, or The Analects of Confucius turn men around, reform them, transform them, and set their faces towards the better life?

This then is the master fact: The Bible makes men. The poet Alexander Pope, himself an unbeliever, when asked to define a Christian, made this brief answer: "A Christian is the highest style of man." If this is true, it is only rational to conclude that it is his devotion to the principles contained in the Holy Scriptures that makes him so.

Chapter 11

Its Influence on National Life

The three world powers today are America and England and Germany, with others forging to the front.[16]

As for England, it was publicly affirmed by Queen Victoria that the Bible was "the secret of its greatness."

As for Germany, at the close of the Franco-Prussian War, it was declared by Père Hyacinthe[17] to his people that the reason for their calamitous defeat lay in the fact that they were irreligious, while every German soldier had a Bible in his knapsack.

As for America, its whole constitutional fabric is permeated with the teachings of the divine Word.

Of the other nations now rapidly coming to the front, Japan stands foremost. A dozen years ago a Japanese student asked to be enrolled as a member of the church to which I minister. His name is still on its roster. At the conclusion of his post-graduate course at Columbia University, he received the degree of Doctor of Laws. On the eve of his departure to his native country, he left with me his Japanese Bible as a token of

---

16 *Why I Believe the Bible* was originally published in 1917, when things were very different with these nations.
17 Père Hyacinthe was a famous French preacher and theologian.

friendship. I said to him, "Are you going back to advocate the teachings of that Book?"

His answer was: "I love my country. We want your light, your freedom, and your constitutional rights. We want your Western civilization, and I am satisfied that we cannot have it without taking the Bible along with it." That man is now one of the primary and best-known publicists of Japan, and he remains a firm believer in the Word of God.

The consummate fruit of Christianity is civilization. Take a map of the world and draw a line around the territory that has felt the benign influence of the gospel, and you will have enclosed substantially all its light, humanity, and civilization. The lands which you drew a line around are significantly known as "Christendom." This enclosed area is so called because it embraces every region that, having the Scriptures, has prospered under the luminous shadow of the cross. All outside is darkness and barbarism. All within is light and progress. This is what the Bible has done; this is what the Bible is doing.

"By its fruits ye shall know it."

It will not be wrong to return more particularly, at this point, to our own country as one of the consummate fruits of the Scripture. It is not enough to recall its original baptism as San Salvador, "The Land of the Savior," nor will it suffice to eulogize our forefathers as Christian men. The important fact is that the great principles which underlie our government are Bible principles, and they do this so distinctly that our welfare and destiny are involved in our loyalty to them.

The first of these principles is the rights of man, as formulated in the word *equality*, which is the antithesis of caste. The proposition that differentiates our republic not only from all monarchies but also from all other constitutional governments is laid down in the Preamble of the Declaration of Independence as a self-evident fact: particularly, "all men are created equal, that they are endowed by their Creator with certain unalienable rights, that among these are life, liberty, and the pursuit of happiness." Where did that proposition come from?

At the time when the King James Version of the Scriptures was translated, the doctrine of human equality was less real than a vision of the night. Man as man was scarcely thought of. The people were mere flies and earthworms in the sight of His Majesty and the Titled Orders. It is true that the Magna Carta had been signed some centuries before, but the Magna Carta was no symbol of popular rights. The people had no part or lot in it. In fact, there were no people. The barons made their demands on John Lackland, and his answer was simply a concession of baronial rights.[18] The last man to recognize the people was the royal patron of the King James Version. He had exiled Andrew Melville for insisting on the right of public assembly in Scotland. All praise to Melville who on that occasion dared to pluck his sovereign by the sleeve, saying, "Sire, thou dost forget that there hath been born in Scotland of late a king before whom all the Stuarts must doff their bonnets." And when James inquired who that might be, he calmly answered, "King People, Sire!" To the truth of that prophecy, the constitutional government of Great Britain bears testimony in these better days.

As far as the rights of the people have been realized in these centuries, it is in persistence in the teaching of Scripture that every man is represented as being by virtue of his divine birthright the equal of his fellow man. The manifesto of Paul on Mars Hill, *[God] hath made of one blood all nations of men for to dwell on all the face of the earth,* struck the keynote for the future (Acts 17:26). The bell that rang from Independence Hall, "All men are created equal," was but a clear, distant echo of it.

The second of the great ideas which underlie our republic

---

18   John, King of England (1166–1216), was the youngest of four sons of King Henry II. He was nicknamed John Lackland because he was not expected to inherit significant lands.

is the sanctity of law, as formulated in the word *government,* which is the antithesis of personal independence.

The basis of social order is the just recognition by every man of the rights of his fellow men. One who dwells alone in the desert may do as he pleases, but if another joins him, his personal freedom is reduced in that he is now free only to do that which does not trespass on the freedom of the other man. As still others arrive, they form a compact; that social compact is government, whose basis is law.

The Scriptures stand for law. The two great ethical symbols of the world are the Ten Commandments and the Sermon on the Mount. Out of the former has grown the jurisprudence of all civilized nations; out of the latter has developed the true theory of social rights. The civilization of any people is precisely measured by their regard for the sanctity of law on the one hand and for the well-being of the individual on the other. The best illustration of good citizenship in the history of the world was witnessed in the passion of Christ. He yielded without murmuring to the unjust decree of the authorities, because they were *ordained of God,* and in his vicarious death in our behalf, he set forth the perfect excellence of the Golden Rule: *Therefore all things whatsoever ye would that men should to you, do ye even so to them* (Matthew 7:12).

The third of our great national propositions is the voluntary principle in religion, which is formulated in the word *nonconformity,* the antithesis of which is the uniformity of a political church.

The policy of James I was to require all men to think alike in religious things. He knew only the Establishment. He hated the Catholics, despised the Puritans, and consistently maligned the Presbyterians. He exiled John Robinson and his associates for refusing to pray according to the prescribed form or kneel at the lifting of the mass. "How far that little candle throws its beams!"[19] The time was coming when that same John Robinson would go down to Delft Haven, Holland, and give Godspeed to the *Mayflower* with her cargo of Puritans setting out for the New World in search of freedom to worship God.

To the mind of James, these men were dissenters. The word is a reproach to thinking men, as it is an offense to the gracious God. He puts no thumbscrews on the conscience. We are free to believe or disbelieve; free to obey or disobey and take the consequences; free to be saved or to be lost. He draws us only with the *cords of a man* (Hosea 11:4).

> Though God be good and free be heaven,
>   No force divine can love compel;
> And, though the song of sins forgiven
>   May sound through lowest hell,
> The sweet persuasion of His voice
>   Respects thy sanctity of will.
> He giveth day: thou hast thy choice
>   To walk in darkness still.[20]

The fourth of the great scriptural ideas is one which has not yet found its realization in our republic: that is, the duty of communication, as it is written, *To do good and to communicate forget not* (Hebrews 13:16). This finds its best expression in universal evangelization, which is the antithesis of war.

There are two means of conquest and only two: namely, war and the Word. "Go fight! Go conquer! Go slay!" cry the great powers, and the earth shakes with the footfall of mobilized armies. "Go preach!" says Christ, and behold, *how beautiful upon the mountains are the feet of them that bringeth good tidings* (Isaiah 52:7).

In this great Bible truth, we find the secret of the ultimate

---

19 William Shakespeare, *The Merchant of Venice*, 1596–1599.
20 John Greenleaf Whittier, "The Answer," 1863.

restoration of the world to God. *Put up again thy sword into his place*, said Jesus, *for all they that take the sword shall perish with the sword* (Matthew 26:52). Sin, error, barbarism, and all the forces that make for irreverence and inhumanity are destined to yield to the expulsive power of truth and righteousness, as shadows flee before the rising of the sun. The key to the future is in the promise: *My word . . . shall not return unto me void, but it shall accomplish that which I please, and it shall prosper in the thing whereto I sent it* (Isaiah 55:11).

At the gateway of America stands a colossal statue of Liberty Enlightening the World (the Statue of Liberty). If the Bible were substituted for the torch in the uplifted hand of the goddess of liberty, we would have a true parable of the obligation of our Christian republic to the unchristianized peoples of the earth. We speak of our country as "God's country," and surely he has not dealt in this manner with any people; but the principles which dominate our national life are like loaves which are best enjoyed by sharing them with others. Therefore it is fitting for us to send the Bible, the divine source of our prosperity, to the uttermost parts of the earth. So in the spirit of a larger patriotism, we shall justify the otherwise selfish sentiment of our national hymn:[21]

> Our fathers' God, to thee,
>   Author of liberty,
> To thee we sing;
>   Long may our land be bright
> With freedom's holy light.
>   Protect us by thy might,
> Great God, our King![22]

---

21 This is different from the "The Star-Spangled Banner," which was written in 1814 by Francis Scott Key and declared the national anthem by Herbert Hoover in 1931.

22 Samuel Francis Smith, "My Country 'Tis of Thee," 1832.

Chapter 12

Its Place in the Forefront of Events

The keynote of modern progress was struck by Wycliffe, AD 1380. In the museum at Prague, there is a symbolic picture of the Reformation as a fagot-fire (burning bundle of sticks) to which Wycliffe is applying the torch. His watchword was, "Let us get back to the Bible!" The search warrant which Christ himself placed in the hands of the people when he said, *Search the scriptures,* had been snatched away and appropriated by the pope and the hierarchy.

As far as the people were concerned, the Bible had long been a closed book, kept in cloisters or chained to the high altars of cathedrals. When given to the multitudes, it was recited in an unknown tongue. Wycliffe said, "I will translate the Scriptures into the vernacular, so that every ploughboy may read them as he toils among the furrows." On being published, his Bible was immediately placed in the Index Expurgatorius.[23] He himself was persecuted to the death, and by order of the Council of Constance, his bones were burned and their ashes cast upon

---

23 A list of books to be censored before they can be read by Roman Catholics. It was later included in the general Index Librorum Prohibitorum or Index of Forbidden Books.

the river, which carried them to the sea. But the keynote of Protestantism had been struck: "A true Bible and an open one!"

In that same picture of the bonfire at Prague, there is another man blowing the flame. This is Luther, who nailed the ninety-five theses of Protestantism to the chapel door at Wittenberg, AD 1517. While still in monastic orders, he had happened upon a volume of the Scriptures. He knew them only as a forbidden book. He read it secretly until he came to the place where it is written, *There is none other name under heaven given among men, whereby we must be saved* (Acts 4:12).

Meanwhile, he had grown lean and haggard. The friars saluted him with "Good appetite, brother Martin," but the dining hall had no charms for him. He returned again and again to the forbidden book. Presently he read: *By the deeds of the law there shall no flesh be justified* (Romans 3:20). The peril of his spiritual state overwhelmed him. At last he came upon the words, *What the law could not do, in that it was weak through the flesh, God sending his own Son in the likeness of sinful flesh, and for sin, condemned sin in the flesh* (Romans 8:3). Then the light began to break through!

He went to Rome. Great were his anticipations, but a sore disappointment awaited him. He had hoped to see the holy brethren serving God in vows of poverty and self-denial; he found a company of priests with round bodies and reddish faces, dwelling in sumptuous halls and imbibing the stores of famous wine cellars. He looked for haircloth but found purple and fine linen, wealth, splendor, and luxury. Here were churches, marvels of architecture, adorned by the art of Raphael and Titian. Here were Bibles in Latin, chained to the high altars. Here, where he looked for humble friars, were arrogant bishops devoted to ambition and political intrigue. They smiled at him as a simple rustic.

Once as he was saying Mass, a neighbor elbowed him with

the remark, "While thou art saying it once, we could repeat it seven times." Ill at ease he chose penance. He would climb the Sacred Stairway on his knees. Halfway up he seemed to hear a voice saying, *The just shall live by faith* (Romans 1:17). The day broke! He stood erect, a believer in the Scriptures and in Christ as his only Savior. Out of that experience came the indomitable courage with which he forever defended his faith until, in the presence of secular and ecclesiastical potentates, he exclaimed, "Here I stand, I cannot do otherwise. God help me!"

As Protestants, we stand as Luther did for an open Bible and a free conscience to interpret it. In the forty years prior to the Reformation, no less than sixteen hundred "heretics" were burned at the stake. All of them died for the crime of doing their own thinking. A man has a right, as far as other men are concerned, to be a heretic at will or an infidel if he chooses, since each must answer for himself before God. Alone I was born into the world; alone I am called to face the responsibilities and progression of life; alone I must pass through the valley of the shadow of death, and alone I must finally stand before the judge of all.

The men who have taken this position have been pioneers of progress through the ages. The Bible and progress go hand in hand. The motto of the Papal Church is *semper idem,* "always the same." The temperature of Saint Peter's at Rome is said to be constant. But true religion is *nunquam idem;* that is, it moves with the moving world. There are two important facts that never change: One is Christ, who is *the same yesterday, and to day, and for ever* (Hebrews 13:8), but the world is constantly catching new glimpses of the beauty of his face. The other is the Bible, which remains unaltered and unalterable, because it was divinely sealed with seven seals. There is no appendix, no addendum. Nevertheless, as John Robinson said, there are "new lights ever bursting forth from it." These are the two unchangeable facts: Christ and the Bible, between which the church moves onward in new enterprises to cumulative conquests of faith.

Such is our religion as outlined by Providence in the logic of events. Its only pontiff is Christ, whose name is above every other which is named in heaven or on earth (Philippians 2:9-10). Its only hierarchy is the procession of torchbearers who go with his gospel to illuminate the dark places of cruelty and the habitations of death, and the procession of reapers who come from yellow fields, bringing their sheaves with them. Its only Book is that which was written by holy men as they were moved by the Holy Spirit. Its only creed is that which is framed from the Scriptures by men sitting at the Master's feet. Its grandest cathedrals are the lives of righteous men who realize their kingly birth and destiny, know their rights, and dare to carry on. Its most fervent litany is this: "From all tyranny of mind, conscience, and heart, good Lord deliver us!" Its most sublime music is the breaking of chains and the attendant anthem:

> All hail the power of Jesus' name!
> Let angels prostrate fall.
> Bring forth the royal diadem,
> And crown him Lord of all.[24]

We are now prepared to lay down this proposition: *The Bible is at the forefront of every great movement making for light and humanity and civilization throughout the world today.*

1. In supporting that proposition, let us affirm at the outset that the Bible stands most important in maintaining the authority in domestic life. This is because all happiness centers in the home, and all civilization radiates from it. No picture compares

---

24   Edward Perronet, "All Hail the Power of Jesus' Name," 1780.

with the love in a cottage where parents and children gather around the family altar. Blessed are they who can look back through the panorama of years to the training of such a home. Its memory never fades. I am sorry for the man whose deepest heart does not respond to the solemn emotion found in Robert Burns's "The Cotter's Saturday Night":

> The cheerfu' supper done, wi' serious face,
>   They, round the ingle, form a circle wide;
> The sire turns o'er, with patriarchal grace,
>   The big ha'Bible, ance his father's pride:
> His bonnet rev'rently is laid aside,
>   His lyart haffets wearing thin and bare;
> Those strains that once did sweet in Zion glide,
>   He wales a portion with judicious care;
> And "Let us worship God!" he says with solemn air. . . .
>
> Then, kneeling down to Heaven's Eternal King,
>   The saint, the father, and the husband prays:
> Hope 'springs exulting on triumphant wing,'
>   That thus they all shall meet in future days,
> There, ever bask in uncreated rays,
>   No more to sigh, or shed the bitter tear,
> Together hymning their Creator's praise,
>   In such society, yet still more dear;
> While circling Time moves round in an eternal sphere.

What makes a home like that? The Bible! The world knows that this assures the joy and sanctity of domestic life.

2. The Bible also leads the way in the betterment of social life. It stands for law and order and all the conditions that make a community a desirable place to live.

If you were on your way westward in search of a desirable place to settle down and "grow up with the country," and if, in your loneliness and uncertainty, the open door of a wayside house should disclose a Bible, you would instantly say, "I can safely sleep here tonight." And suppose that the next morning on awaking you should hear the ringing of church bells, wouldn't you say, "This is the village for me"?

In this regard, it may be well to recall the words of James Russell Lowell:

When the keen scrutiny of skeptics has found a place on this planet ten miles square, where a decent man can live in decency, comfort and security, supporting and educating his children unspoiled and unpolluted, a place where age is reverenced, infancy respected, womanhood honored, and human life held in due regard; when skeptics can find such a place, only ten miles square, on this globe, where the Gospel of Christ has not gone before, and cleared the way and laid the foundations and made decency and security possible, it will then be in order for the skeptical literati to move thither and ventilate their views.

The Bible builds no saloons, no brothels, no gambling dens; it builds instead schools and hospitals and institutions that make for the uplifting of all sorts and conditions of men. This is a fact so obvious and universally conceded that it is quite unnecessary to dwell upon it.

3. Furthermore, the Bible is at the forefront of our industrial life. One day last week, I watched from my study window many thousands of striking craftsmen marching by. In that procession I observed a few American flags and a considerable number of others inscribed with the ominous slogans of socialism, but not a single one that expressed the remotest acquaintance of the industrial ethics set forth in the divine Book of the Law. Yet these honest toilers – foreign born with scarcely an exception

– should be advised of the fact that except for Christ and the Bible, there would be no Third Estate (caste of commoners), no wage system, or any possibility of striking against oppression in our country or anywhere else.

At the beginning of the Christian era, the only toiler was a bondslave with no remuneration except his meager board and keep. Then came the Carpenter of Nazareth with his great manifesto: *The labourer is worthy of his hire* (Luke 10:7). During the succeeding years, the Bible, which was and is the Carpenter's Book, has carried the same manifesto to the limits of the civilized world, so that Christendom today marks the boundaries of the recognized rights of the laboring class.

No doubt there are still wrongs to be righted, but point me, if you can, to any land without the Bible where the protest of the employed against the arbitrary rule of the employer is permitted in any form. Could the builders of the pyramids strike against their taskmaster with his whip of scorpions? Are there any strikes in Senegambia or Tierra del Fuego? If not, why not? Because the Sun of Righteousness has not risen upon them! The Carpenter with his Book has been marching through the centuries and urging the square deal of the Golden Rule, so that wherever he has gone, capital and labor are beginning to see face to face, but nowhere outside of Christendom is there any such condition of things. Nowhere else is there a gleam of promise of the day "when man to man the world o'er, shall brothers be."[25]

4. Further, the Bible, as we have already seen, is at the forefront of the world's national life. The reason we foreigners are here – for we are all foreigners to a greater or lesser extent – is that we believe America to be the best country the sun ever shone on. It is a refuge for the oppressed of all nations, and they are

---

25 Robert Burns, "A Man's a Man For A' That," 1795.

coming from everywhere. Why do they turn their steps this way? They are fleeing from the lands of a chained Bible to the land of an open Bible! They are escaping from the oppression of darkness to mingle with a people whom the light of truth makes free.

The youngest boy in our public schools knows that Columbus discovered America in 1492, but he does not know perhaps that America was not peopled for a hundred years after that. This is a noteworthy fact. What happened in the interim? A tremendous cataclysm that turned the world upside down. A movement for the unchaining of the Bible. If Luther had not issued his theses against the closing of the Scriptures, there would have been, so far as we can see, no scattering of the night. If Holland had not fought for an open Bible, the *Half Moon* would never have sailed this way.[26] If Cromwell and the Roundheads had not championed the right of personal interpretation, the *Mayflower* and her gallant crew would never have been heard of. The people came, and the people are still coming, because a closed Bible means tyranny and oppression, while an open Bible insures life, liberty, and the pursuit of happiness.

Our country is a Christian country. It was founded, we repeat, on the principles laid down in the Ten Commandments and the Sermon on the Mount, and it has developed along the lines marked out in the divine Book of the Law. In the year 1777, a strange thing happened. The Revolutionary War had stalled the output of the printing presses, and the result was a famine of the Word. Congress was petitioned to relieve the situation, and what did Congress do? It authorized the importation of twenty thousand Bibles from Holland to be distributed among the people! Would Congress go that far today? I fear not. But this is what our forefathers thought of the Book of the Law.

But if it is true that our government is founded on the

---

26   The *Halve Maen* (Half Moon) was a Dutch East India Company ship that sailed into what is now New York Harbor in 1609.

Scriptures, that its history and jurisprudence, its freedom and prosperity, its proud memories and bright prospects are all interwoven with the truths and precepts of Scripture, will you tell me how it happens that the politicians in many of our states feel free to discriminate against the Bible? The General Assembly of New York recently turned down a bill calling for the reading of the Bible in the public schools. Meanwhile, some of the schoolhouses on Manhattan Island are open every evening of the week for the propagation of anarchy and socialism. The pernicious doctrines of Karl Marx are allowed, but the Bible is taboo. Spinsters are permitted to discuss eugenics and birth control, but religion is banned. Ex-convicts are welcomed, but Christ is ruled out. And all the while, the Christian community makes no practical protest, but complacently foots the bills!

5. Finally, the Bible leads the march in international affairs. And now you are pointing across the sea and saying, "Behold the war of Christian nations! Is this the best that an open Bible can show for itself?" The point is well taken. But Christian nations are no more perfect than Christian men. The inconsistency would not be noted if it were not for the universal conviction that the prevailing war is not the outcome of loyalty to the Scriptures but in violation of them.

And will you tell me, in passing, why you point derisively at France and England and Germany and Russia and Austria without a word about Turkey and other Ottoman states? Because you are aware that the Bible teaches peace while the Qur'an teaches war. Because all the world knows that frightfulness is expected of a non-Christian nation while the very opposite is expected of those that have the Bible and live by it. Thus, obviously your acrid criticism becomes a glowing tribute to the Word of God.

But there are influences at work that will presently make

an end of war. What and where are they? With one consent we say, the principles of justice and humanity and universal harmony which are laid down in the Scriptures. All courts of arbitration are built upon those principles. Even in the grapple of the nations, the Bible forges to the front. I hold in my hand a khaki Testament, just received from the Belgian firing line. On its flyleaf are these words:

> August 25th, 1914
>
> I ask you to put your trust in God. He will watch over you and strengthen you. In this little Book, you will find guidance when you are in health, comfort when you are in sickness, and strength when you are in adversity.
>
> Roberts

This message from the beloved "General Bobs" is being read by the men in the trenches, and the gospel, which it commends, is thus making a *reductio ad absurdum* (reduction to absurdity) of this and every war.

It will be heard from in the Council of the Great Powers, which will soon assemble to determine the conditions of peace. An invisible Presence will be there, an overtowering Figure, beside whom kings and kaisers and czars and emperors will dwindle into insignificance. The last word in that council will be spoken by the divine Man with the Bible in his hand. The Prince of Peace will ultimately bring in the truce of God.

Let us therefore have confidence in the Bible. When the ark of the covenant was taken by the Philistines at Ebenezer, the prosperity of Israel went with it. Old Eli sat by the gate, awaiting the news of battle. A messenger came running with his clothes torn and ashes on his head. Eli asked, *What is there done, my son? And the messenger answered and said, Israel is fled before the Philistines, and there hath been also a great slaughter among the people, and thy two sons also, Hophni and Phinehas, are dead, and the ark of God is taken. And it came to pass, when he made mention of the ark of God, that he fell from off the seat backward by the side of the gate, and his neck brake, and he died* (1 Samuel 4:16-18).

Woe the day when God – symbolized by this ark of the covenant – shall lose its place in the loyal hearts of God's people. But that shall never be. The divine truthfulness stands pledged to the eternity of the divine Word until it shall accomplish the purpose of God.

For so runs the promise: *As the rain cometh down, and the snow from heaven, and returneth not thither, but watereth the earth, and maketh it bring forth and bud, that it may give seed to the sower, and bread to the eater: so shall my word be that goeth forth out of my mouth: it shall not return unto me void, but it shall accomplish that which I please, and it shall prosper in the thing whereto I sent it* (Isaiah 55:10-11).

Thus it is written and thus it must be, for the mouth of the Lord has spoken it.

Chapter 13

It Is Christ's Book

The storm centers of religious history are Christ and the Bible.

As to this Jesus, who is called the Christ, who is he? Is he what he claimed to be – the only begotten Son of the Father or a trickster and a fake? This is the Chateau Hougoumont,[27] around which the Waterloo of the centuries has been waged, for it is understood that if Christ could be disposed of, the fabric of Christianity would vanish into thin air.

And when the controversy has not been about Christ, it has centered in the Bible. What is this old Book? Is it what it claims to be – *God-breathed* – or is its distinction due only to certain venerable associations (2 Timothy 3:16)? Are there any clear characteristics which lift it out of the category of other books? Can it be received with confidence as an "infallible rule of faith and practice," or are those who so regard it merely a sort of fetish-worshippers? Is it the Truth, or does it only contain truth, that is, more or less of it? What do you think?

These two are the controversial centers of our religion as they ought to be, and they are really and substantially one. The

---

27 Chateau Hougoumont was the key point of defense where Wellington battled Napoleon on June 18, 1815.

porch of Solomon's temple was held up by two brazen pillars, the names of which were *Jachin*, or strength, and *Boaz*, or continuance. A Jew going up to the temple, faint and heavy-hearted, felt his vigor and confidence renewed as he gazed upon these massive pillars with their beautiful capitals of lily work. In this way, Christ and the Bible uphold our religion. While they remain, it is safe. And they are destined to abide forever because *the mouth of the Lord hath spoken it.*

It is significant that both Christ and the Bible are characterized as *the Word of God*. How indeed could God reveal himself to men than by his Word? He is seen in nature but not clearly. It would be difficult for a man to look so far "through nature up to nature's God" as to be able to say, "*Abba, Father!*" He would be much more likely, standing amid the bewildering glories of the earth and overarching heavens, to cry aloud in desperate desire, "O God, if thou art or wherever thou art, speak to me!"

And God has spoken: As it is written, *In the beginning was the Word, and the Word was with God, and the Word was God. And the Word was made flesh, and dwelt among us* (John 1:1, 14). Language is the medium through which we become acquainted with each other. You are discovering what sort of person I am by what I am saying now. In like manner God makes us acquainted with himself through his Word. The incarnation was the articulation of the divine mind. We are not surprised, therefore, to hear the incarnate Son claim to be a full and complete revelation of the Father. On one occasion *Philip saith unto him, Lord, show us the Father, and it sufficeth us. Jesus saith unto him, Have I been so long time with you, and yet hast thou not known me, Philip? he that hath seen me hath seen the Father; and how sayest thou then, Show us the Father? Believest thou not that I am in the Father, and the Father in me?* (John 14:8-10).

But this was not enough. God must speak further if he

would make himself heard by all mankind through all succeeding ages. Jesus in his earthly life was hemmed in by a narrow environment of time and space. His ministry lasted only three years, during which he canvassed only a small portion of a small province in a remote corner of the globe. Should he content himself with the healing of a few folks and preaching to some thousands of stiff-necked and unregenerate Jews? No, all nations and all centuries would be groaning and laboring together for him. The Word must traverse the world. The Sun of Righteousness must go forth as a bridegroom out of his chamber, and no generation must be hidden from the light of it. But how should that be accomplished? By the written Word, which is the reflex of Christ, his universal and perpetual shining forth. Through the Scriptures, he is made known to all generations, to the uttermost parts of the earth, and to the remotest end of time.

The pages of Scripture, like the leaves of the Tree of Life, are *for the healing of the nations* (Revelation 22:2). They flutter in the winds of heaven, bearing the tidings of redemption to those who sit in darkness and the shadow of death. If Christ is to reign universally, it is because, under the dispensation of the Spirit, the information is being successfully carried through the instrumentality of the written Word. This is the weapon of the kingdom; for it is written, *The sword of the Spirit, which is the word of God* (Ephesians 6:17). Thus the Bible is the complement and counterpart of Christ. The two Words are one; and this binomial Word is a complete, continuous, and universal revelation of God.

Do they, then, *stand or fall* together? Nothing is said of their falling. Christ and the Bible stand together, and standing thus, they stand forever; neither can fall.

We hear much today about a "Christocentric" religion. The word has a very attractive look and sweet sound, but there is reason to fear that under certain conditions, it may be made to serve Christ himself erroneously. If it is used to emphasize the need of a more profound regard for the teaching of our Lord and Savior, let us cordially assent to it, but if ever it serves as a mere ploy for rejecting or minimizing Christ's unswerving loyalty to the Scriptures, then we are bound to regard it with suspicion. For nothing is more certain than Christ himself being the very first to reject a Bibleless gospel, no matter what sweet adjectives were attached to it. The ultimate test of devotion to him is faith in the sum total of his teaching in every way.

Let us now observe what the Bible has to say about Christ, and then what Christ has to say about the Bible. It will thus appear how they stand together as complementary, each to the other.

To begin with, the Bible is more than a mere biography of Christ. To say that its purpose is exclusively to outline the scheme of salvation in its narrow sense may furnish a takeaway phrase but not a complete statement of fact. There are many things in Scripture which have no direct bearing on the way to escape from the penalty and power of sin. And whatever the Bible contains, whether theological, ethical, or scientific, is absolutely true. Thus it is written, *All scripture is given by inspiration of God, and is profitable for doctrine, for reproof, for correction, for instruction in righteousness: that the man of God may be perfect, thoroughly furnished unto all good works* (2 Timothy 3:16-17), that he may have well-rounded and symmetrical equipment for life in every way.

It is correct to say, however, that the golden thread running through all the Scriptures is Christological. Their central theme is Christ. This is true both of the Law and the Prophets.

The common title of the Scriptures among the Jews was "The Law and the Prophets."

The moral law as delivered from Sinai is a schoolmaster to lead sinners to Christ. The ceremonial law in all its rites and symbols points directly to him. Its local center was the tabernacle which, from the brazen altar at its door to the ark of the covenant in its remote holy of holies, was everywhere a type of him. Its calendar center was the Day of Atonement, when every occurrence, from the robing of the priest in fine linen clean and white to the sending away of the scapegoat to Azazel, was expressive of him.

The same may be affirmed of the prophets. The beginning of prophecy was the *protevangelium* (first good news) in Eden, when God said to the serpent, *I will put enmity between thee and the woman, and between thy seed and her seed; it shall bruise thy head* (Genesis 3:15). As years passed and men forgot God and lapsed into the abominations of the heathen, Abram was called out of Ur of the Chaldees and chosen to preserve monotheism and hand it down through succeeding generations until the advent of Christ. To him was the promise given: *I will bless thee, and make thy name great; . . . and in thee shall all families of the earth be blessed,* a promise to which Jesus himself ascribed distinct messianic importance (Genesis 12:2-3).

The psalms of David are so full of Christ that they furnish much of the material for our Christian hymnbooks. Isaiah for a similar reason is called the evangelical prophet. He foretells Christ as a child, a teacher, a wonder-worker, a Man of Sorrows, a vicarious sacrifice – one who by dying triumphed over death to live forever as the Mediator and Advocate of penitent souls. Daniel saw the great world powers rising and flourishing and passing away to make room for the universal dominion of the Messiah. The last of the prophets, Malachi, in the gathering gloom of the long Egyptian night of four hundred years which intervened between the two Testaments, waved his torch, crying, *The day cometh, . . . the Sun of righteousness [shall] arise with healing in his wings* (Malachi 4:1-2). Thus Christ is discernible everywhere in the Law and in prophecy, like the theme or undertone of an oratorio; therefore, it would be obviously impossible to keep the Bible and disregard Christ.

What now, on the other hand, was the attitude of Christ toward the Bible?

To begin with, he was familiar with it. He learned it by memory in his boyhood, and ever after made it his infallible rule of faith and practice. In each of his three temptations in the wilderness, he used it as an effective guard against the adversary. When urged to change stones into bread to satisfy his hunger, he answered, "Nay, I cannot! For I remember what my mother taught me out of the Book: *Man shall not live by bread alone, but by every word that proceedeth out of the mouth of God*" (Matthew 4:4). When urged to cast himself down from a pinnacle of the temple to prove his Godhood by his superiority to natural laws, he answered again, "Nay, I cannot! For I remember what the Bible says: *Thou shalt not tempt the Lord thy God*" (Matthew 4:7). And when urged finally to avoid the agony of the cross and accept the world's sovereignty in return for a single act of homage rendered to its *de facto* prince, he answered, "I cannot! For the Book says, *Thou shalt worship the Lord thy God, and him only shalt thou serve*" (Matthew 4:10). Thus in every case the Bible was his foundation. *It is written* was enough for him. And blessed is every one of his followers who can defend himself in like manner with the sword of the Spirit, which is the Word of God.

1. But now, to be more specific, Christ declares the Scriptures to be true. He does not hesitate to call them "truth." He does not say that they "contain" truth but that they are the Word of God. In his priestly prayer on behalf of his disciples, he pleads, *Sanctify them through thy truth: thy word is truth* (John 17:17). A follower of Christ ought to be willing to follow him in his endorsement of the Scriptures as much as in faithful service.

He affixed his seal to the story of the deluge, saying, *As in the days that were before the flood they were eating and drinking, marrying and giving in marriage, until the day that [Noah] entered into the ark, and knew not until the flood came, and took them all away* (Matthew 24:38-39). He believed in the story of the destruction of the cities of the plain by fire and brimstone from heaven, in the healing efficacy of the brazen serpent, in the turning of Lot's wife into a pillar of salt, and in Jonah in the whale's belly. He thus gave an explicit assent to the so-called fables of the Old Testament which are so abhorrent to many modern critics. He was better advised than most of our biblical expositors, respecting the real facts on the question of inerrancy, and knowing all, he did not hesitate to endorse the entire trustworthiness of those very portions of Scripture that are most vigorously attacked today.

As to the Pentateuch, Jesus not only endorsed its trustworthiness but also repeatedly ascribed its authorship to Moses, as when he asked, *Did not Moses give you the law?* (John 7:19). And with respect to Deuteronomy, which the destructive critics have pronounced to be a substantial forgery, he placed a peculiar sanction upon it. In his temptation in the wilderness, the words with which he repelled the adversary on each occasion were from Deuteronomy. A critic of the modern school has recently written, "The Bible is no better than a mass book for stopping a bullet, nor as good as holy water for putting out a fire." But our divine Master evidently thought otherwise when he made this book of Deuteronomy an effective shield against the approaches of the tempter, putting out his fiercest fire with water from Siloam's brook.

As to the scientific propositions of the Scriptures, our Lord endorsed the origins of Moses and those early records on which rest the ethnology and philology of our time. The assault on the science of the Scriptures is by no means recent. Julian the

Apostate (Roman emperor AD 361–363) attempted to cast reproach upon it. But while the theories of falsely so-called science have passed through no end of kaleidoscopic changes along the pathway of the centuries, the Bible continues to hold its own. And when such scientists as Dana, Guyot, Faraday, and others too numerous to mention assert its substantial truth, we do not feel called upon to withdraw or qualify faith in it.

As to the historical parts of the Old Testament, our Lord put his distinct sanction upon them, and the recent research of archaeologists furnishes a cumulative confirmation. Professor Sayce, a pioneer British Assyriologist and linguist, affirms that no less than seventy-seven events in Assyrian history as given in Scripture have been corroborated by recent excavations. In any case, however, the important fact is that Jesus Christ never called these historical records into question, but positively as well as tacitly placed his endorsement upon them.

As to prophecy, the pastor of one of our evangelical churches is reported to have said, "I know of no one passage in the prophets which can certainly be said to point to an event beyond the near future of the writer." If this is true, then Jesus was mistaken when he said, *Moses ... wrote of me* (John 5:46), and again, *The scriptures ... are they which testify of me* (John 5:39). He found the Old Testament full of predictions about himself and his redemptive work, with predictions pointing to history in the remote future, even to the events of the last days.

As to these particular parts of the record which have been most bitterly attacked by the modern school of critics, it should be enough to mention our Lord's reference to and implied endorsement of the stories of Adam and Eve, Abel, Noah and the flood, Abraham, the destruction of Sodom, Lot's wife, Jacob's ladder, Moses and the burning bush, the manna, the brazen serpent, David, Solomon, the Queen of Sheba, Elijah raising the widow's son, Elisha and Naaman, and Jonah.

As to the story of Jonah in the whale's belly, our Lord risked the validity of his entire ministry upon it. The Jews clamored for a sign; he said, *There shall no sign be given . . . but the sign of the prophet Jonas: for as Jonas was three days and three nights in the whale's belly; so shall the Son of man be three days and three nights in the heart of the earth* (Matthew 12:39-40).

Yet we are told that the story of Jonah is a fable, pure and simple, no more trustworthy than that of Aladdin and his wonderful lamp. To what an inferior anticlimax would this reduce the confident challenge of Jesus, as if he had said, "As surely as Aladdin worked wonders by rubbing his magical lamp, so surely shall I rise again from the dead and bring life and immortality to light!"

But there are those who are unwilling to concede that Christ's authority was conclusive upon this point. They say, "He had his limitations."

It is granted that our Lord, in subjecting himself to the conditions of our earthly life, was pleased to lay aside the full exercise of his divine powers; he held his omniscience, omnipotence, and omnipresence in temporary cessation, but never such that he could not summon them at will at any moment (Matthew 26:53).

His limitations, whatever they may have been, were certainly not such as to expose him to the liability of error or to the danger of uttering an untruth. To assert this would be to say a monstrous thing, for it would reduce our divine Teacher to the level of Muhammad and Joseph Smith. It is manifest that this position is impossible to any follower of Christ. One of the fathers of modern unbelief was indeed pleased to say on a certain occasion, when reminded of a divine statement, "I am not willing to receive that upon the authority of any such person as God." It is related also that in a recent meeting of evangelical ministers, the question was asked, "If Moses did not write the Pentateuch, why did Jesus Christ say that he did?" A voice replied, "Because he knew no better." It is incredible, however, that such views should be entertained by any of the sincere followers of Christ.

As if to anticipate the current objection to his testimony on the ground of human limitations, our Lord asserted that the Father was himself responsible for his teaching. He said, *I can of mine own self do nothing* (John 5:30), and again, *My doctrine is not mine, but his that sent me* (John 7:16). He also said, *I have not spoken of myself; but the Father which sent me, he gave me a commandment, what I should say, and what I should speak . . . even as the Father said unto me, so I speak* (John 12:49-50). Again he said, *The word which ye hear is not mine, but the Father's which sent me* (John 14:24). So, to question the teaching of Jesus with respect to the Scriptures is not merely to doubt the statement of one who was subject to human limitations, but it is also to call into question the truthfulness of the living God.

2. Then observe the eloquent silence of Jesus with respect to all those alleged errors and discrepancies which so vex the souls of certain of our learned folk. Did he know that these blunders were to be found in the sacred pages? If the Mosaic cosmogony (story of origins) is false, how is it that he uttered no word against it? And why did he not denounce those blasphemous psalms which are "too horrible to be read" in some of our modern pulpits? How is it that he did not expose the falsity of those prophecies concerning himself, which "have never been fulfilled and never can be because their time has gone by"?

Surely it is not too much to suppose that Jesus was an honest man. He seems to have been a fervent hater of shams and acts of deception, lying frontlets and phylacteries, false traditions of the elders, and deceptions of every sort. Is it possible that his eyes were not as clear in this particular area as those of our recent biblical scholars? Or was his soul not as sensitive as theirs with regard to these dreadful things in Scripture? Was he unscrupulous or merely ignorant? Must we put the most severe limitations upon his knowledge, assuming that he knew no better than to let these errors pass unchallenged, or must we challenge his genuineness? In either case we could scarcely receive him as our divine Savior and spiritual guide. We would surely turn from him to the guidance of these wiser men.

3. Let us further note how Christ risked his entire work on the truth and trustworthiness of Scripture. At the very outset of his ministry, he went into the synagogue at Nazareth and opened the scroll of Isaiah at the place where it is written, *The Spirit of the Lord G*OD *is upon me; because the* LORD *hath anointed me to preach good tidings unto the meek; he hath sent me to bind up the brokenhearted, to proclaim liberty to the captives, and the opening of the prison to them that are bound; to proclaim the acceptable year of the* LORD (Isaiah 61:1-2; Luke 4:18-19).

And, having read this passage, he said to his audience, *This day is this scripture fulfilled in your ears* (Luke 4:21).

If we follow him through the three eventful years of his ministry, we shall find him again and again, in the same manner, pledging the truth of his teaching and the genuineness of his work on the formal decree of the Holy Word.

After his resurrection, while walking with certain of his disciples along the way to Emmaus, *beginning at Moses and all the prophets, he expounded unto them in all the scriptures the things concerning himself* (Luke 24:27). It would be interesting to know the substance of that expository sermon. We may be quite sure that he unfolded the meaning of ancient rites and symbols, as well as messianic predictions, in the light of things which had recently happened at Jerusalem. This was in agreement with his previous utterance: *One jot or one tittle shall in no wise pass from the law, till all be fulfilled* (Matthew 5:18). Thus it is written and thus it must be.

So Christ planted himself on the absolute truth of Scripture and risked the integrity of his work on it. And what was good enough for our Lord and Master ought to be sufficient for those who profess to follow him. He stood as a constant witness to the unqualified truth of the Scriptures, always turning to them as a Court of Final Appeal in verification of his divine nature and advocacy work; he said, *Search the scriptures; for in them ye think ye have eternal life: and they are they which testify of me* (John 5:39).

I do not see, therefore, how it is possible to detach the written Word from the incarnate Word. They stand together. They are unreservedly loyal to each other. How could it be otherwise when they are both revelations of the same God?

Attention is now called to a striking parallel between the two Words in the following particulars:

First: Christ as the incarnate Word and the Scriptures as the written Word are both called "the Truth" and "the Word of God."

Second: They are both theanthropic: that is, divinely conceived and humanly born. As such, the divine and human are inseparably blended in them. Christ was conceived by the Holy Spirit and born of the Virgin Mary, but in partaking of his mother's humanity, he in no wise inherited her sin. In like manner the Scriptures were written by certain men as they were moved by the Spirit of God, and in this case it is also claimed that the divine, human product was free from human imperfection. The features of Jesus doubtless bore a distinct likeness to those of his mother, just as the pages of the Holy Word are marked by the mental characteristics of their human penmen. In neither case does this resemblance prevent that absolute faultlessness that belongs to any word of God.

Third: It is only in the original that either the incarnate or written Word can be called inerrant. We have heard the higher critics saying, "What is the use of affirming inerrancy of an original writing which is not in existence? The theory that there were no errors in the original text is sheer assumption, upon which no mind can rest with certainty. We must take the Scriptures as we have them, without reference to a hypothetical original, which no living man has seen." It is a poor rule, however, which cannot be made to work both ways. No living man has ever seen the incarnate Word. There is no accurate portrait of him in existence, certainly not if the Scriptures are unreliable. Every version of Christ that is produced in the life and character of Christians is full of imperfections. Nevertheless, we do believe that the original Christ, who for a brief period of thirty-three years lived among men and then vanished from sight, was *holy, harmless, undefiled* (Hebrews 7:26), precisely as the Scriptures were in their original form.

Fourth: Notwithstanding all errors in translating, the Word in both cases remains in such substantial perfection as to be effective for the accomplishment of its purpose. A special providence has kept before the eyes of all generations the image of an immaculate Christ. A like special providence has so guarded the transcription of the written Word that we may confidently hold it to be an infallible rule of faith and practice. Neither the incarnate nor the written Word, as we have them, can lead a soul astray, but will infallibly carry the believer at last to heaven's gate.

To recapitulate: Our Lord believed the Bible, spoke of it as "the Truth" and as "the Word of God," and preached it, practiced it, and risked the integrity and success of his redemptive work upon its truthfulness. He affirmed its truthfulness as he stood for its record of creation, the destruction of *the cities of the plain,* Jonah's adventures on the way to Nineveh, and other portions that are most frequently called into question. He commissioned his disciples to preach the Bible to the uttermost parts of the earth, thus making it the determining factor in the problem of his kingdom. He never uttered a single word or syllable to indicate that he thought it to be anything but true from beginning to end.

How shall we account for his consistent loyalty to the Scriptures? And how shall we explain that eloquent silence of his with respect to its alleged errors? We face a threefold alternative. First, there were no such errors in Scripture. Second, the errors were there but Christ was not aware of them. Third, he was aware of them but did not choose to explain.

In the first case, the Scriptures must of course be regarded as true. In the second case, if Christ was not aware of the alleged errors, then the destructive critic of our time is wiser than he and therefore more worthy to be our spiritual guide. In the third case, if he knew there were such errors in Scripture and did not tell, he was not an honest man.

Chapter 14

Excursus: A Hypothetical Story[28]

Jesus: His Book

As I entered the synagogue, a Man had just risen to read the lesson of the day. It was obvious that he, though clad in homespun, was no common man, and by his reverent handling of the Book, it seemed that he regarded it as no common book.

The lesson was from one of the messianic prophecies of Isaiah: *The Spirit of the Lord GOD is upon me; because the LORD hath anointed me to preach good tidings unto the meek; he hath sent me to bind up the brokenhearted, to proclaim liberty to the captives, and the opening of the prison to them that are bound; to proclaim the acceptable year of the LORD* (Isaiah 61:1-2).

Having read that far, he closed the Book and began to say, "*This day is this scripture fulfilled in your ears*" (Luke 4:21). In the discourse that followed, he advanced the stupendous claim that he, this Man in homespun, was the long-awaited Messiah *that many prophets and kings have desired to see . . . and have not seen them* (Luke 10:24). As he proceeded, the eyes of all that

---
28 Injection of unauthentic matter. This chapter is an imaginary situation by the author.

were in the synagogue were fastened on him. But the claim and the claimant were so amazingly at odds that murmurings began to be heard. "*Is not this the carpenter's son?*" (Matthew 13:55). Presently they rose up with one consent and thrust him out.

I followed and, on joining him, asked, "Who art thou?" He answered, "I am *the only begotten Son, which is in the bosom of the Father* before the world was (John 1:18). I am Immanuel: that is, God dwelling among men. I am he of whom it is written, *In the beginning was the Word, and the Word was with God, and the Word was God. And the Word was made flesh, and dwelt among us*" (John 1:1, 14).

Then I asked, "What is the Book?"

He answered, "This also is the Word of God, the Scriptures; *Search the scriptures; for in them ye think ye have eternal life: and they are they which testify of me*" (John 5:39).

But, not knowing the credentials of the Book, I continued. "How may I be assured that this is the true Word of God?"

Therefore he said, "By its fruits thou shalt know it. Come with me down the centuries, and I will show you what this Book has done, is doing, and can do."

We presently came to the door of a humble home, at which he knocked, and on being admitted, he raised his hands in benediction saying, "Peace be within this house!"

On a table in the center of the living room lay the Book from which the good man of the house had been reading with his family gathered around him. By the light in their eyes, I knew that this was a Christian home, where husband and wife were bound by an imperishable tie, and the children were knit together by filial love.

As I looked inquiringly toward my Guide, he said, "All homes are thus happy when governed by the principles which are written in the Book."

"But is there no sorrow here?"

EXCURSUS: A HYPOTHETICAL STORY

"Oh yes. Once and again the shadow of death has crossed the threshold, but the Book gives *beauty for ashes, the oil of joy for mourning, the garment of praise for the spirit of heaviness* (Isaiah 61:3). The members of the household do not sorrow as those that are without hope; there is a rainbow in every tear, for when they say, 'Farewell,' they only mean, 'until we meet again.'"

And I said within myself, "Surely a book that radiates such happiness must have come from God."

He then brought me to a workshop. As we entered, I saw men toiling at the bench. Some of them were lazy; some made light of their tasks, and some spoke angrily of other workmen and conspired against their employers. These were embittered and discontented with their lot. But others applied themselves industriously to the business in hand, thinking of labor less as drudgery than of serving others.

I asked my Companion, "What makes the difference?"

He replied, "The principles which are written in the Book. For therein is the primal law: *In the sweat of thy face shalt thou eat bread* (Genesis 3:19); and there also is written the Golden Rule: *Therefore all things whatsoever ye would that men should do to you, do ye even so to them*" (Matthew 7:12).

And again I said within myself, "A book that teaches us to live and let live, to be industrious and content, and to regard the welfare of others while making the most of ourselves is worthy of the mind of God."

He led me from the workshop to an exchange, where capitalists were dealing in bonds and mortgages and planning great enterprises. Here also I perceived a difference. Some of them had worshipped the yellow god so long that they had grown yellow with the jaundice of gold. They were sons of the horseleech, with hands like outstretched talons and fevered lips crying, "Give! Give!" They were money-sharks – miserly, extortionate – as they ground the faces of the poor. They were shrewd bargainers, bankers, and ambidextrous over-reachers. They were dying of "the sacred hunger of gold" but didn't know it. But others were equally rich and enterprising but openhanded, magnanimous, and ever ready to communicate. They believed in fair dealing and consented that the laborer is worthy of his hire. For them, wealth had no value except for what it could do, and the best it could do was to make its possessor rich toward God. In the use of their wealth, they regarded themselves as stewards, holding all in trust and at the divine call.

"Is this," I asked, "the teaching of the Book?"

He answered, "It is. The treasure that lies buried in the bosom of the everlasting hills is the Lord's, and whatever he has committed to these stewards is a solemn trust to be used for the advancement of his kingdom of truth and righteousness on earth and in doing good as they have opportunity unto all men."

And again, I reflected that the presumption is in favor of the superhuman origin of a book with such an influence among the children of men.

We then visited an institution of learning, where many students were bending over their books, books of art and science and philosophy. I knew that these students sought after truth, but would they find it? Some were pursuing the knowledge of earthly things as an end in itself and not as a means to an end, and by their knit brows, they were finding that *much study is a weariness of the flesh* (Ecclesiastes 12:12). The Book of all books was neglected by them, and they *by wisdom knew not God* (1 Corinthians 1:21). Others, while knowing the value of all truth, searched the one Book for a solution to the great problems in the issues of eternal life. These put the emphasis on character and usefulness and immortality, and they seemed to be living in the hope of living forever. For them, time was a school of preparation for eternity, and death the great commencement.

"It is a wonderful Book," said I to myself, "that can overarch

EXCURSUS: A HYPOTHETICAL STORY

life with promise and lofty hope and aspiration." And a voice beside me seemed to be saying,

> There is the lamp whose steady light
>   Can guide the traveler in the night;
> 'Tis God's own Word; its beaming ray
>   Can turn a midnight into day.[29]

My Guide said, "We will now visit a hospital," but even as he spoke, the skies were overcast, and the earth began to rumble with the footfall of armies. Kings and rulers could be heard taking counsel together and saying, "*Let us break [God's] bands asunder, and cast away [his] cords from us.*"

My faith began to shake and tremble. Then a voice beside me said, "Listen!" And lo, above the roar of cannon and clash of steel, I heard a burst of laughter out of heaven! "It is God," he said, "laughing at the folly of the great powers who conspire against him. Behold how he has them in derision! *I will declare the decree: the* LORD *hath said unto me, Thou art my Son; . . . I shall give thee . . . the uttermost parts of the earth for thy possession* (Psalm 2:7-8). Thus it is written and thus it shall be, but alas, with sorrows along the way!"

As we approached the hospital, I saw over its gateway the words *Hotel Dieu*. Ambulances came rolling up with wounded and dying men, and on every ambulance was the symbol of the cross. We entered and walked through the wards of the hospital, and again I saw the symbol of the cross on the arms of the nurses who ministered to the wounded. I asked the meaning of it.

The Man beside me said, "This is the Spirit of the gospel, which is written in the Book. The red cross stands for self-sacrifice on the behalf of others."

A soldier lay on one of the cots, facing the great mystery of

---

[29] Henry John Betts, "There Is a Lamp Whose Steady Light," 1864.

death, but he was unafraid. The Book lay by his side and, as he passed, he murmured, "*I will fear no evil: . . . thy rod and thy staff they comfort me*" (Psalm 23:4).

Then I said to myself, "This is a wonderful Book to live by and to die by."

As we still journeyed we came to a church and entered. The service opened with prayer, and a lesson was read from the Book; the congregation sang, "Blest be the tie that binds our hearts in Christian love."

I asked my Guide if all in this assembly were saints.

"By no means," he answered. "There is not a saint among them.[30] They are all sinners, but sinners saved by grace. They are reaching forth and pressing on, not without much stumbling, toward the prize of the high calling of God. Meanwhile their business is to cooperate with the King in truth and righteousness on earth."

"The wheels of the royal chariot," he continued, "move all too slowly, by reason of the halfheartedness of the King's subjects; but in the fullness of time, he that shall come will come and will make no delaying, and on that day every knee shall bow before him."

On a map suspended over the pulpit, I observed a red line, drawn around a third portion of the world. "The part thus enclosed," said my Companion, "is called *Christendom* because the glory of the Book has fallen over it. Within that charmed circle are all the light and humanity and civilizations of the world. Beyond it lie darkness and the shadow of death."

"How is it," I inquired, "that Christians have not carried the Book to those regions beyond?"

"They have been so negligent of their commission," was his answer, "that after the lapse of nineteen centuries, there are still twelve hundred millions of people who have never seen the

---

30 Obviously, the Guide in this story is using a different meaning for the word *saints* because Scripture does refer to sinners saved by grace as *saints*.

Book or heard its good news. Meanwhile, vain is their prayer, '*Thy kingdom come,*' for the gospel must first be proclaimed throughout the whole world; then shall the end be."

We next entered a great assembly hall. Above the chair of the presiding officer were the words, *Liberty, Equality, Fraternity.* A man was on his feet presenting a report that concluded with these words: "Resolved, that there is no God." The report was adopted with one consent. The streets were immediately filled with a surging mob who echoed the cry, "There is no God!" On their shoulders they carried a prostitute to Notre Dame, where she was enshrined above the high altar as the goddess of reason. The terror had begun! There were wagons hastening with victims to the guillotine. The gutters were running red. The newborn republic was tottering to its fall!

Then in a moment we seemed to be transported to another legislative hall. On a bell above the doorway was inscribed the legend: "Proclaim liberty throughout the land and to all the inhabitants thereof." As we entered, an honorable man was invoking the blessing of God. On the desk of the presiding officer lay the Book that was to furnish the laws and jurisprudence of this republic.

I asked, "What will be the outcome? Will the republic last?"

His answer was, "As long as its people are true to its landmarks." And as we came away, there was an anthem full of promise sounding through the air:

> Our fathers' God to thee,
>   Author of liberty,
> To Thee we sing.
>   Long may our land be bright,
> With freedom's holy light,
>   Protect us by Thy might,
> Great God our King![31]

---

[31] Samuel Francis Smith, "America (My Country, 'Tis of Thee), 1831.

Then I found myself praying that our country, founded on the principles of right and justice which are written in the Book, might always be loyal to it.

We were now in the open street. Men hurrying by in the mad pursuit of wealth and pleasure seemed unmindful of the great truths of the spiritual life. Some even railed at the Book and profaned the name of God. At this I marveled and would have questioned my Friend about it, but even as I turned, he said, "Farewell," and placing his Book in my hand, he vanished from my sight.

I opened the Book. On its initial page was written, "Jesus: His Book," and on the next, "*Search the scriptures; for in them ye think ye have eternal life: and they are they which testify of me.*"

Finding where the red trail began, I read on and on, following it as one who follows a guide with bleeding feet, until I seemed to stand before a great gate whereon was written this dedication: *The grace of our Lord Jesus Christ be with you all. Amen.*

I recalled the way I had come with my wonderful Guide and the wonderful things I had seen along the way. I said, "The Book that makes happy homes, contented workmen and capitalists who are rich toward God, scholars wise in the problems of eternal life, institutions of mercy, governments founded on the principles of mutual justice, and churches whose spires are like index fingers pointing to a holy and happy heaven is surely the Word of God."

Then I turned once more to the inscription: "Jesus: His Book," and remembered how he knew and loved it, preached and practiced it, and commended it to his followers. He never mentioned it except in terms of highest praise; I held it reverently next to my heart and said, "The Book that was good enough for my Lord and Savior is good enough for me."

Chapter 15

It Is the Church's Book

In Paul's letter to the Christians of Ephesus, he speaks of the church as being *built upon the foundation of the apostles and prophets, Jesus Christ himself being the chief corner stone; in whom all the building fitly framed together groweth unto an holy temple in the Lord* (Ephesians 2:20-21).

A few years ago, the engineers of the Palestine Exploration Fund came upon its original foundations by sinking shafts and opening galleries along the walls of the temple. They were seventy feet below the surface, resting on the rocky slopes of Moriah. At the lowest angle of this temple area, they discovered the cornerstone. It was four feet thick and fourteen feet wide, and the fine original finish of its surface was almost flawless. It is not improbable that the prophet Isaiah had this very stone in mind when he uttered the messianic prediction, *Behold, I lay in Sion for a foundation a stone, a tried stone, a precious corner stone* (Isaiah 28:16).

It thus appears that the most important place in the church, deepest down and most fundamental, is reserved for Christ. The *rock* to which Christ referred when he said, *Thou art Peter, and upon this rock I will build my church* (Matthew 16:18) was not Peter, but Peter's good confession: *Thou art the Christ, the Son of the living God* (Matthew 16:16). If this is questioned, let Peter himself be heard:

> *Ye also, as lively stones, are built up a spiritual house, an holy priesthood, to offer up spiritual sacrifices, acceptable to God by Jesus Christ. Wherefore also it is contained in the scripture, Behold, I lay in Zion a chief corner stone, elect, precious: and he that believeth on him shall not be confounded. Unto you therefore which believe he is precious: but unto them which be disobedient, the stone which the builders disallowed, the same is made the head of the corner, and a stone of stumbling, and a rock of offence, even to them which stumble at the word, being disobedient.* (1 Peter 2:5-8; cf. Acts 4:8-12)

1. But if Christ is the chief cornerstone of the church, the Bible is its foundation. Paul says, *Ye . . . are built upon the foundation of the apostles and prophets,* this being a common and well-understood phrase used to designate the Scriptures in those days.

I wonder whether the destructive critics who are engaged in undermining the popular faith in Scripture are aware of what they are doing. *If the foundations be destroyed, what can the righteous do?* (Psalm 11:3). The only Christ we have is the Christ who is revealed nowhere else but in the Scriptures. To impair their credibility is to attack the only historical witnesses that bear testimony to our religion. Some of these destroyers are among the professed followers of Christ, but surely they do not follow him in this, for as we have seen, he never uttered a word in opposition to the absolute truth of the Bible but, on the contrary, was always ready to vindicate and uphold it.

But how do the Scriptures serve as the foundation of the

church? In furnishing all that is necessary for its organization and effectiveness in every way, Herbert Spencer says that two things are necessary for a working church: namely, creed and religion.

The Scriptures furnish the creed or system of truth; they also furnish the religion or mode of worship. The latter, as given by inspiration, is intensely simple. The beauty of holiness is the service of the heart, its form being relatively of slight importance. To ask, "When I offer my prayers, shall I sit or kneel or stand upon my feet?" is precisely like the question asked of Sir Thomas More by his executioner: "Sir, does your head lie right upon the block?" to which he answered, "It matters naught about my head as long as my heart is right." Let us abide by Scripture in this matter, avoiding all unnecessary form and ceremony, which is but abundance of naughtiness. *For whatsoever is not of faith is of sin* (Romans 14:23).

But something more than creed and religion is needed in the making of a church. For one thing, we must have a perfect code of morals. And this we find in the Ten Commandments and the Sermon on the Mount, plus the personal example of Jesus as the ideal Man.

We also need a program of life, or a plan of campaign, and this is clearly marked out in the Scriptures. What is the business of those who belong to the church? It is to *seek ye first the kingdom of God, and his righteousness* (Matthew 6:33). As we walk along the street, we mingle with two classes of people who look alike, but they are really separated by an immeasurable gulf. On the one hand, some are wholly absorbed in the pursuit of wealth, pleasure, or other personal profit; they neither know nor apparently care to know anything beyond the things of this present life and are forever hastening to the grave, stooping downward as they run. On the other hand, not a few believe in the coming of the King and intend to do all in their power to hasten it. They are also engaged in bread-and-butter work, but the things of the kingdom are supreme, and their prime purpose is to hasten its coming on earth and in the lives of men.

2. The church is not only founded on the Scriptures, but it is also their storehouse, holding them in trust for safeguarding and worldwide dissemination.

In one of Paul's letters, he advises Timothy, his successor in the pastorate of the Ephesian church, to *hold fast . . . that good thing which was committed unto thee keep by the Holy Spirit which dwelleth in us* (2 Timothy 1:13-14).

The reference is distinctly to the *paratheke*, or body of revelation, which had been *once delivered unto the saints* (Jude v. 3). Therefore, the church is characterized as *the pillar and ground of the truth* (1 Timothy 3:15). The word *church*, or *ekklesia*, means "called out." The church is a body of men called out of the world for the specific purpose of preserving and utilizing this deposit of scriptural truth until the whole world shall become acquainted with it.

The original germ or nucleus of Scripture was the moral law, together with the civil and ceremonial law, which complemented it. God's jealousy for the acceptance of his Word is shown by his command to the Levites: *Take this book of the law, and put it in the side of the ark of the covenant of the* Lord *your God, that it may be there for a witness against thee* (Deuteronomy 31:26). In the course of time, there was added to this original nucleus a further set of revelations known as the New Testament, and these, together with the preceding ones, constitute the Scriptures as they are committed to us.

The Jews were set apart as a church or chosen people for the express purpose of keeping their Scriptures flawless and passing them on to the coming ages. In the course of Paul's great argument on justification by faith, where he shows that

Jewish rites and ceremonies had no power to save, this objection is interposed: *What advantage then hath the Jew?* to which he answers, *Much every way: chiefly, because that unto them were committed the oracles of God* (Romans 3:1-2). This then was the singular privilege and prerogative of the Jews; they were chosen to be custodians of the Word. Alas, they proved faithless to their trust. They rejected their oracles and crucified the Hope of Israel. Therefore, God *[removed their] candlestick out of [its] place* so that every wandering Jew in the world today is a living monument of the divine jealousy for the Scriptures as revealed truth (Revelation 2:5).

The Christian church, as direct successor of the Jewish church, has a similar mission. To it are entrusted the Scriptures for safekeeping, for exposition, and for propagation to the uttermost parts of the earth. This trust is expressed in missions. To save souls is a divine prerogative, but to disseminate truth, the gospel of the Scriptures through which souls are saved, is the distinct business of the church. When that is heeded, God promises to do the rest. A clear understanding of this fact with a corresponding zeal in missions brings us closer to the fullness of times. When Christ was asked by his disciples for a sign of his second coming, he answered, *This gospel of the kingdom shall be preached in all the world for a witness unto all nations; and then shall the end come* (Matthew 24:14).

The body of truth thus deposited with the church has been placed in the special care of its ministers.

In the Jewish church, the prophets were charged with the special duty of safeguarding the oracles and teaching them. In time, there arose within their number a new order known as *scribes,* that is, transcribers of Scripture. They were the biblical experts of those days who assumed to be able to rightly divide the Word of Truth. It was not long, however, before they began to take undue liberties with the Word for which our Lord denounced them, saying, *Full well ye reject the commandment of God, that ye may keep your own tradition* (Mark 7:9). And again: *Woe unto you, scribes and Pharisees, hypocrites* [mask-wearers]*! for ye shut up the kingdom of heaven against men: for ye neither go in yourselves, neither suffer ye them that are entering to go in. Ye blind guides, which strain at a gnat, and swallow a camel. Ye serpents, ye generation of vipers, how can ye escape the damnation of hell?* (Matthew 23:13, 24, 33).

All this because they were false to their oracles, adding to and subtracting from them, overlaying them with their traditions and thus diminishing their commission to safeguard and distribute them.

The call to the Christian ministry is a divine call. It is a summons to the sacred trust of protecting, defending, and distributing the truth as contained in the Scriptures, and fidelity to that commission is solemnly pledged in its ordination vows.

In the early church there were ministers who were unfaithful to their trust. Paul was moved to warn Timothy against such false teachers, saying they *creep in* among the people to make shipwreck of faith. He warned the young pastor of Ephesus against their deceptive inroads, and with pathetic earnestness urged him to be faithful: *O Timothy, keep that which is committed to thy trust* (1 Timothy 6:20).

Are there such false teachers among us? It is an open secret that not a few have infiltrated the evangelical pulpits where they, sometimes brazenly but more often with covert cleverness, not only undermine the written Word but also deny the incarnate Word. What do they care about ordination vows? Honesty and truthfulness are cast to the winds. "Oaths are but straws!"

What is the result? The question is frequently asked, "Why are there so few candidates for the ministry?" The wonder is that there should be any candidates at all when there are so many ministers and theological instructors who reduce the gospel to *nil*. Why should a young man consecrate his life to preaching when there is nothing to preach? In Germany, where the pulpits are largely given over to rationalism, the supply of candidates is less than one-third what it was fifty years ago. In our own country, there is a smaller but still lamentable falling off. Why? Inquire at the doors of Yale, Harvard, Princeton, Cornell, and other great institutions of learning, notably our state universities. In these universities, rationalistic science and philosophy are taught in direct contrast to the Scriptures. Is it to be expected that young men will be moved by such instruction to devote their lives to a profession which is solemnly pledged to the teaching of propositions which they must not believe in?

A further result is the breaking up of the foundations of common morality. Faith and conduct go together. One who is more liberal than the doctrine of Christ must be broader than the moral law. It would not be just to say that all liberals are on the wrong side of all current questions of reform. But it is quite within bounds to say that ministers and laymen who stand by the evangelical faith can always be depended on to support the formal decrees of the Sabbath, temperance, the marriage relationship, and every other proposition which concerns the welfare of society. When the question of opening our saloons on Sunday was pending in our legislature, the state of New York was ransacked to find ministers who would advocate it. A few were found, eleven to be exact, and naturally all liberal. Not one among them stood for the integrity of the written and incarnate Word of God.

It is worthwhile for those who thoughtlessly denounce creeds and clamor for ethical sermons to remember that truth and morality walk hand in hand. There is no sound and dependable morality which does not find its base in obedience to revealed truth. To abandon that truth, as a whole or in any essential part, is to loosen the sanctions of right and righteousness, *for as [a man] thinketh in his heart, so is he* (Proverbs 23:7).

3. But this is not all. The church is not only founded on the Scriptures and put in charge over them as a solemn trust, but as already intimated, it is also directed to teach them to the uttermost parts of the earth.

The command is to *preach the word* (2 Timothy 4:2). The church, we repeat, is not expected to regenerate men; God himself does that, but every member of the church is, up to the full measure of his influence, charged with the responsibility of carrying the inspired Bible with its glad tidings to the regions beyond until it has reached the last man.

The church has been blamefully slow in realizing the responsibility of taking the good news of Christ to the world. Sporadic efforts have been made to bring the nations to a saving knowledge of religion in other ways, but God's way is the only way. The Spirit works through the Word for the salvation of men. Therefore, preach the Word! When that is done, we can safely and hopefully leave the results with God.

Chapter 16

It Is Everybody's Book

One of the most convincing arguments for the divine origin of the Scriptures is their singular adaptation to the needs of all sorts and conditions of men.

Here is a book for young and old, for rich and poor, for lofty and lowly, and for wise and unwise. This Book is for all who feel the burden of sin and the need of One who has power on earth to forgive sin; it is for all who realize the cramping limitations of this present life and long for a vision of life hereafter; it is for all from every tribe and nation of the children of men. There is no part of human experience where this Book does not touch us. In pain, sorrow, poverty, discouragement, loneliness, and death, it lends a hand to uplift and support us. Wherever we are, whatever we do, however we suffer, as Coleridge said, "The Bible finds us."

This is due in large measure to the fact that it reduces all the profound problems which it undertakes to solve to their simplest terms. And it does this by scrupulously avoiding the terminology of the schools and appealing directly to common sense.

1. Take, for example, the doctrine of the atonement. What

labyrinths of argumentation have been constructed about this vital truth. Listen to the objections: "Is it to be supposed that God would scourge his only begotten Son?" "Can the innocent suffer for the guilty?" "Is there any purifying value in suffering and death?"

Ask the child at your knee to answer these objections, for indeed the argument must ultimately be solved by the intuition of innocence; for it is written, *Except ye be converted, and become as little children, ye shall not enter into the kingdom of heaven* (Matthew 18:3).

"Will the Father scourge his beloved Son?" Surely not unless some appropriate end requires it, or unless the Son himself, in view of that high purpose, should with a glad heart consent to it. But listen to his words: *Lo, I come: in the volume of the book it is written of me, I delight to do thy will* (Psalm 40:7-8).

"Can the innocent suffer for the guilty?" What a question! The innocent are all the while and everywhere suffering for the guilty: kings for their rebellious subjects, parents for their wayward children, and everybody for his sinning ancestors. Nor is there anything finer in human nature than the voluntary suffering of one for another; that is sympathy, which Webster defines as "the quality of being affected by the affection of another." If it is true that we are by nature the children of God, what sort of a God would he be who did not suffer vicariously for us? By this token, the highest note in the history of humanity is struck at Calvary. Here is the supreme expression of divine love. It is just like God. It is just what we should expect of him.

"Is there any purifying value in suffering and death?" That depends. It must not be overlooked that there is a covenant to be reckoned with in these premises, and to that covenant there are three parties: namely, God the Father, the only begotten Son, and the sinner (myself). If the Father is willing to send his Son, if the Son is willing to suffer on my behalf, and if I, "the party of the third part," am willing by an obedient and appropriating faith to have it so, where in all the universe is there any who, without impertinence, can object to it?

Such is the simple logic of grace as the Bible teaches it. Sadly, in the process of the years we are prone to drift away from the wisdom that was in the mind of Jesus when he said, *Except ye become as little children.*

> Tell me the story simply,
>   As to a little child,
> For I am weak and weary,
>   And helpless and defiled. . . .
>
> Tell me the story often,
>   For I forget so soon;
> The early dew of morning
>   Has passed away at noon.[32]

2. Consider the doctrine of justification by faith, which Luther called "the determination of a standing or a falling church." It is easy to ask such questions as, "If Christ died for all, then why do I need to believe in him?" or "What saving virtue can reside in faith?"

Ask these questions of the schoolmen and they will lead you into philosophic labyrinths of confusion leading to worse confusion; but go to the Scriptures, and like children in kindergarten, you will be answered by picturesque figures of speech, such as these two:

a. The ground is covered with manna, "white and plenteous as hoar frost." Whosoever will may satisfy his hunger by eating it, but eat he must or famish for lack of it. And Jesus said, *I am*

---

[32] Katherine Hankey, "Tell Me the Old, Old Story," 1866.

the living bread which came down from heaven: if any man eat of this bread, he shall live for ever. . . . Except ye eat the flesh of the Son of man, and drink his blood, ye have no life in you (John 6:51, 53).

b. The water is gushing from the rock at Rephidim. Whosoever will may drink and live. But, though the stream at Rephidim were as broad and deep as the Amazon, a man, refusing to drink, would perish of thirst. And Jesus said, *Whosoever drinketh of the water that I shall give him shall never thirst; but the water that I shall give him shall be in him a well of water springing up into everlasting life* (John 4:14).

Thus, the faith that justifies is represented as a simple appropriation of the benefits of divine grace. It is a glad hand stretched out to take the gift of God. Could any requirement be more reasonable? But we entangle our feet in elaborate misconceptions which prevent us from running the heavenly way.

All that the Scriptures require for our personal salvation is that we accept Christ as our Savior and prove our sincerity by living accordingly. "Only believe!" is the thing we live by. Christ on his cross saves nobody. It is only when Christ crucified is received by faith as "*my* Lord, *my* life, *my* sacrifice, *my* Savior, and *my* all" that I am saved through him. This is not philosophy; it is common sense, and wise men do not hesitate to act upon it.

If we would ever arrive at a solution to these or any other of the great problems of the spiritual life, it must be along scriptural lines. We won't find answers by following blind leaders of the blind in vain excursions into the bewildering mazes of "fixed fate, free will, foreknowledge absolute,"[33] but by pursuing the plain and simple paths marked out for us.

Much of our education is like arboriculture in Japan. An

---

33   John Milton, *Paradise Lost*, 1667.

oak tree is taken from its place on the hilltop where, buffeting the storms, it fastens its roots upon the everlasting rocks and lifts its arms triumphantly in the air. It is reduced by elaborate cultivation to the small dimensions of a plant in a pot. In like manner, as to our attitude toward the great spiritual facts, we move further and further, by a process of mental dwarfing, from the clear and simple light of Scripture into a narrow and inflexible scholasticism which makes us unconsciously but disastrously averse to truth.

It was thus with Nicodemus, to whom Christ presented facts which should have entrusted himself to him at once, but being a rabbi educated in hair-splitting schools of philosophy, he cried, *How can these things be?* (John 3:9).

It has pleased God to give us the Scriptures for our guidance on the pathway of life. They are – as we should expect of a divine chart – so plain that a wayfaring man, however foolish, does not need to err with them. If more were needed, we have it in the aid of the Holy Spirit of whom it is written, *He will guide you into all truth* (John 16:13).

But all guidance is in vain for those who refuse to follow it. Not even common sense, the universal instinct of the race with reference to spiritual things, is adequate for perfect guidance to those who, by willful and habitual wrong thinking, have been diverted from the King's highway. So it is written, *If ye continue in my word, then are ye my disciples indeed; And ye shall know the truth, and the truth shall make you free* (John 8:31-32).

In the interpretation of the divine Word, common sense plus the illumination of the Spirit affords all necessary help. *The true Light, which lighteth every man that cometh into the world* is like a lantern in our hands (John 1:9). If we prefer, we may pursue our journey along the dark and perilous ways of life so absorbed in discussing the science of rays that we stumble into no end of pitfalls. But if we are willing to follow the guidance of the Bible with the aid of the divine Spirit, who both illuminates its pages and anoints our eyes with eye salve that we may see, we shall find the light not only sufficient for each passing hour but also growing brighter and brighter unto the perfect day.

Chapter 17

Its System of Doctrine

Much has already been said about the doctrinal truths of Scripture that this chapter is likely to be brief. However, some additional facts call for emphasis because of their contribution to an argument for the divine origin of the Bible.

1. One of these facts is the comprehensiveness of its doctrinal system.

It would be difficult, indeed impossible, to suggest a single problem in the entire province of religious thought which does not find a satisfactory solution here. And this – considering the antiquity of the Bible, its limited proportions, and the vast diversity of its readers – is a remarkable fact. If this Book is only literature, where is there another like it in all the literature of the world? We find here an answer to all questions about God and immortality, the life here and the life farther on.

2. Another fact worthy of note is that the emphasis that the Scriptures put on these spiritual truths is measured precisely by their relative value in practical life.

For example, the personality of God, together with all those attributes that must combine to form the perfect symmetry of a divine character, is so constantly iterated and reiterated as to leave no room for the faintest shadow of doubt concerning him.

The same is true of the doctrine of sin, which is always yoked with restitution which, unless divinely averted, is sure to follow it.

A similar emphasis is put on the doctrine of justification by faith in Christ and of sanctification through the Word by the power of the Spirit. These are not only vital but also eminently practical truths, because the issues of life and immortality are wrapped up in them.

It is sometimes stated that immortality is not taught in the Scriptures. If true, this would show a fundamental defect, but it may fairly be said that no other doctrine is more clearly imparted. It is not only explicitly taught, but it is also the very premise of all spiritual truth, which is more significant. If death ends all, then the Bible is of less consequence to me, or to any other thoughtful man, than a treatise on wholesome foods. In that case Epicurus was right: "Let us eat and drink: for tomorrow we die."

But the man we meet at the very doorway of the Scriptures has God's breath in his nostrils and is therefore as immortal as God himself. For what can quench this spark of infinite fire? A man created in the divine likeness cannot die as a beast dies. He lives forever! Why do we need labored argument to prove it? Likewise, ask Euclid to postpone his excursion in the higher mathematics until he has demonstrated the axioms, or a professor of applied dynamics to turn aside from his curriculum to prove the existence of force. Wise men waste no time in philosophizing about self-evident facts. Like the writers of Scripture, they assume them and pass on.

But while the more vital doctrines of the inspired Bible are deeply emphasized, the nonessential or less important are more lightly dwelt on, yet not so lightly as to give the impression that any truth is negligible, but only to throw the more significant truths into bolder authenticity. Therefore, room is left for a difference of opinion about certain truths which, while revealed, are not explained because they belong to God.

Such, for example, are "fixed fate, free will, foreknowledge absolute."[34] Here Calvinists and Arminians may agree to differ, because a full understanding of the divine decrees is not necessary to salvation. So, the denominations may excusably be at odds with reference to ecclesiastical forms and political organizations since, important as these may appear, they are not fundamental in the building of life and character. The significant fact is that a sufficient answer is given in the Scriptures to all questions, whether essential or nonessential, which have any bearing whatsoever on life here and hereafter.

3. Another fact in this connection has already been referred to: namely, the universal adaptation of scriptural truth. In one of Augustine's sermons, he remarks that "the Scriptures are so deep that an elephant can drown in them, and shallow enough to be forded by a lamb." The problems considered are indeed profound, but their solution is adjusted to the ability of all sorts of men.

Contrast, for example, the scriptural teaching about the being and nature of God with the scholastic method of clarifying the same truth. The students in our theological seminaries are drilled in the ontological, cosmological, and teleological modes (philosophies dealing with metaphysics, astronomy, and evolutionary purpose) of demonstrating that the world is not an incidental gathering of atoms but a creation with a Creator behind it. Open the Bible and immediately the whole argument confronts you: *In the beginning God*! If the Bible had been made

---

34   John Milton, *Paradise Lost,* 1667.

for theologians, it too might have dealt in long phrases with multisyllabic words. But this is the universal highway, and no such polysyllabic terms as *ontological, cosmological,* or *teleological* shall be found there. The King's road was not made for philosophers but for wayfaring men.

The Bible does not attempt even a formal definition of God. This was left for the Assembly of Westminster theologians who, summoning their highest wisdom, produced this splendid labyrinth of words: God is a spirit (What is Spirit?), infinite (What is infinite?), eternal (What is eternity?), unchangeable (Think of unchangeableness, if you can!) in his being (As to "being," let Herbert Spencer speak: "Life is a definite combination of heterogeneous changes, both simultaneous and successive, in correspondence with external co-existences and sequences"), wisdom (Who can comprehend omniscience?), power (Will you measure omnipotence with a yardstick?), holiness (The white solar ray), justice (Let Shylock and Portia cross lances here), goodness (*As far as the east is from the west*), and truth.[35]

Here Pilate speaks for all the schools: "*What is truth?*" Thus, the most reverent attempt to define the great mystery ends in a succession of teratologies (science of monstrosities). Now open the Bible and hear the words of the great Teacher: *After this manner therefore pray ye: Our Father* (Matthew 6:9).

Enough! God is defined. The plummet of philosophy can sound no deeper depths; the dreams of prophecy can reach no loftier heights, and a little child can understand it.

4. It remains to consider the important fact that the Bible alone, of all the so-called sacred books of the world and of the centuries, so presents the numerous truths of religion that they can be arranged in a coherent system.

Who ever heard of the doctrinal system of the Qur'an or of

---

35   *The Westminster Shorter Catechism,* www.apuritansmind.com/westminster-standards/shorter-catechism/.

the Zend-Avesta or of The Analects of Confucius? There is no claim of consistency here, but consistency is the crown jewel of the Scriptures; the ecumenical creeds of Christendom are the logical expression of our scriptural faith. The many divisions of the evangelical church – however far apart they may be in minor points of order – are all agreed as to these customs. A heretic in one of these denominations is a heretic in all. To deny that God is holy, that man is a sinner, or that the only atonement is worked by the God-man is to be an Ishmaelite among all the tribes. The vital truths are thus recognized as a system whose doctrines hold together like the links of an anchor chain. Break one link and your ship is adrift. For this reason, a man's safety lies not in accepting so much of Scripture as may please him, but in adhering to the whole without cutting anything out. For its truths go together, as if intended to be, in George Herbert's words, "a necklace of pearls for the adornment of the bride of God."

Chapter 18

Its Moral Code

The average man is inclined to do right, but obviously he must have a reliable rule to live by. Where shall he find it? *Can tradition supply such a rule?* Is it enough for one to do as his fathers were accustomed to doing? On the contrary, the law of heredity, when applied in the sphere of ethics, is a ball and chain rather than a door opening into life. There is many an inebriate who justifies his loss of self-respect on the ground that a strain of alcoholism runs in his veins. But if he would remove his father's decanter from his own cupboard and put up a brave fight for the recovery of his manhood with a firm reliance on divine help, he would surely win out. The sour grapes, which our forebears have eaten, cannot relieve us of personal responsibility. Every man must answer for himself before God.

Is it safe, then, to follow prevailing custom? Shall we do as others do – attend church because church-going is popular or run with the multitude to do evil, as the case may be? Conformity is a weak guide at best, since it changes with shifting time and circumstance. In some portions of Switzerland, goiters are so common that a man who does not have such an enlargement is called "goose-necked." One is sure to go wrong who merely follows the precept: "When you are in Paris, do as Parisians do."

Or shall we follow conscience? If we cannot find a standard by comparing ourselves with ourselves, shall we look for it within ourselves? No, let no man boast of being a conscientious man, since conscience may be seared by sinful habit as with a hot iron. It may be twisted out of its normal direction as the magnetic needle is deflected by the iron in a ship's hull. Saul of Tarsus persecuted the Christians in all good conscience. Philip II followed his conscience in expressing a desire to "ride up to the bridle in Protestant blood." It is not enough, therefore, to follow the inward voice.

Where, then, is the standard? Nowhere, unless God himself, the God of right and righteousness, shall reveal it. *If any of you lack wisdom, let him ask of God, that giveth to all men liberally, and upbraideth not; and it shall be given him* (James 1:5). The answer to that asking is found in the Scriptures, and a clear understanding of the Scriptures is provided by the Spirit of God. One of the official functions of the Holy Spirit is to regulate the conscience in that way.

The prime objective of prayer is to arrive at that which the perverted and unaided conscience cannot give, particularly a clear expression of the divine will. We are bound to do right, not merely what we believe to be right. We are bound to live as God in his Word directs us to live. It is not enough to say that our lives are conformed to the requirements of conscience; they must be conformed to the divine law as an enlightened conscience enables us to see it. This enlightenment is through the divine Word, precisely as a skipper corrects his compass by taking an observation of the stars. This Word, therefore, is ultimate, because through it God speaks to those who are inclined to hear and obey him.

In the Ten Commandments, which were the original nucleus

of the Old Testament (Deuteronomy 5:31), we have a brief compendium of the moral law. One offense makes a man an outlaw, just as the deviation of a planet from its orbit by as little as a single inch makes it a wanderer in infinite space. Hence the need of a remedy for sin; inasmuch as *all have sinned, and come short of the glory of God* (Romans 3:23).

This remedy was provided under the old covenant, the prophecy of Christ, which was known as *the hope of Israel* (Acts 28:20). No sooner had Adam sinned than he was pointed to Christ as the seed of woman who would come in the fullness of time to *bruise [the serpent's] head* (Genesis 3:15). When Cain killed his brother, he was informed that *sin lieth at the door* (Genesis 4:7). Thus, the Savior was revealed, and progressively revealed, in the prophecies of the Old Testament for the deliverance of ancient sinners, so that all who believed in the coming Christ might live by faith in him.

Then the day broke. The Messiah came and with him another covenant, which is characterized as "a new covenant" by reason of the clearer emphasis that it puts on the same covenant of grace which was originally made with Adam for all the children of men. The seed of woman was at hand with his face set steadfastly toward the cross on which he was to bruise the serpent's head. In him we behold *the Lamb [of God] slain from the foundation of the world* (Revelation 13:8).

He said that he had come not to destroy the law but to fulfill it – to pay the ransom due by bearing our sins in his own body on the tree. Thus, he magnified the law while designing a highway over which the lawbreaker might enter into life. Never was justice so vindicated as in the vicarious death of Christ, by which it is made manifest that God can be just and also the justifier of the ungodly through which a man can be just with God.

Nor was the law ever so honored as in his life and teaching. The

Sermon on the Mount is his exposition of the Ten Commandments, and in that sermon there is no pacifying of sin. As an exposé it burns like acid; it blisters like fire; it searches out the secret imaginations of the heart. It proclaims that the law is good, and that it must be kept even to the last jot and tittle of it. *If ye love me, keep my commandments* (John 14:15)

In following him, we shall find him honoring the law by presenting it to its simplest terms. *Thou shalt love the Lord thy God with all thy heart, and with all thy soul, and with all thy mind. This is the first and great commandment. And the second is like unto it, Thou shalt love thy neighbour as thyself. On these two commandments hang all the law and the prophets* (Matthew 22:37-40).

Out of these great commandments proceeds the rule of social service. All right-thinking men and women are desirous of making this world a better place to live in. We hear the cry for help on every side. How shall we answer it? What shall we do for the army of ne'er-do-wells, for the lazy and ignorant, for the permanently impoverished 10 percent, for God's poor and the devil's poor, for the sick and suffering, and for widows and the fatherless? Hear the bitter cry!

We get together in sociological conventions. We collect statistics, compare communities, and measure ourselves against ourselves. We write about civic reform and prison reform and reforms without end. We build schools, hospitals, and reformatories. We contribute for soup kitchens, employment bureaus, art exhibits, entertainments, and university buildings. So far, so good; but all this falls infinitely short of the requirements of the situation. Our measurement of the case is too narrow and superficial. We are treating man simply as an unfortunate animal for whom death ends all. We are estimating his needs by the cry of his appetites. He is hungry, let us feed him. He shivers, let us clothe him. He cannot distinguish between a chromo and a masterpiece of Raphael; therefore, let us cultivate his aesthetic nature! Is man then no better than a sheep? Is he nothing more than a stomach and its appendages? Is the problem of his welfare to be solved by the argument of a full dinner pail? Is physical comfort the sum total of happiness?

God be praised for all that is being done to alleviate the sufferings of the poor and destitute, but the Epicurean tendency of current sociological effort is greatly to be lamented. We blame the sickly sentimentalism of women who carry jellies and bouquets to Murderers' Row, but is it better to supply the present needs of the unfortunate while ignoring the more profound needs of their spiritual nature? Is this our boasted progressivism? Is it not rather a reversion to a barbaric type? "Let us eat and drink," said Epicurus, "for tomorrow we die!"

But we do not die tomorrow; we live on and on through interminable tomorrows. Man is more than an animal; he is a child of God, created in the divine likeness and facing the blessed possibility of a divine heritage. His life here is only a handbreadth, so that however bad his present afflictions may be, they endure but for a moment, while his life hereafter stretches on forever and ever.

We err, therefore, in measuring immortal needs by physical standards. We fall infinitely short of philanthropy in seeking to meet an eternal need by the betterment of temporal conditions. Man is indeed an animal in that when he hungers, he must eat, and when he shivers, he must be clothed. But somehow in our charity we must get eternity into the reckoning. No true kindness fails to see beyond the narrow horizons of the here and now, *for what is a man profited, if he shall gain the whole world, and lose his own soul?* (Matthew 16:26).

Is there a perfect standard of such comprehensive humanity? Is there a satisfactory gauge by which we may measure our efforts, *as we have therefore opportunity, . . . [to] do good unto all men* (Galatians 6:10)? Is there a good work anywhere in history by which all other works may be measured?

Yes, open the Bible and behold the cross! Here is the ultimate standard of philanthropy. The cross stands out in history as a divine announcement of the only effective plan for the deliverance of the whole man. It saves the soul by blotting out sin. On the one hand, it disinfects memory by erasing the past; and on the other hand, it glorifies hope by preparing the soul to meets its destiny. Thus, it saves a man, body and soul, for time and eternity. For the man who finds salvation in Christ is put in the way of a holy endeavor to surrender himself like a man. Bring him to Calvary, and you insure his temporal as well as his spiritual good. He is no longer content with wretched pursuits and companionships; the squanderer is ashamed of his recklessness and becomes ambitious to live as an honest man among men. His whole life is revolutionized by a vital comprehension of the gospel of Christ.

It is a small matter to feed one who is doomed to the gallows. Esau may be willing to trade his birthright for a mess of pottage, but too bad for the Jacob who became a party to it. An artist, desiring to paint a picture of The Prodigal's Return, engaged a beggar to sit as his model. The next day at the appointed hour, the man appeared dressed in his best. His appearance was improved, but he was more worthless than before, since he had become unfit to serve as a model for the prodigal. It is proposed in some quarters by those who are engaged in philanthropic effort to treat all prodigals in this way – to furnish them with soap and water, a change of clothing and something to eat, and leave them in the far country. No! No! Let us get the wanderer well on his way to his Father's house, knowing that once there, he shall have food and clothes in plenty and sit at a well-filled table, wearing the best robe.

This is the method of the Scriptures as illustrated by the

philanthropic Christ. He healed the sick and alleviated the miseries of the poor and suffering, but these were mere by-products of his redemptive work. His face was set steadfastly toward the cross, and on his way he consistently preached the higher life of reconciliation with God. Let the mind that was in Christ Jesus be also in us.

Chapter 19

Its Plan of Salvation

The Bible is like a drama with a distinct purpose running through it from beginning to end. It is clear, progressive, and crucial. A thin red line as distinct as the theme of an oratorio can be traced from the first evangel, or gospel, at the gateway of Paradise to the last vision of the Apocalypse where the redeemed saints are represented as glorifying God, for their robes are washed and made white in the blood that cleanses from all sin (Revelation 7:14).

We follow this crimson trail through chronicle and psalm and prophecy with ever-increasing interest, perceiving more and more in the light of multiplying altars and watch fires that some supreme event approaches. Suddenly there is a gush of music from the Judean hills: *Glory to God in the highest, and on earth peace, good will toward men* (Luke 2:14). The *denouement* (final outcome) is at hand! Yonder on Calvary, the Hope of Israel, the Desire of all nations, dies in anguish, bearing the world's sin in his own body on the tree. Then another burst of music from the heavenly heights: "Worthy art thou to receive honor and glory and power and dominion forever and ever, for thou wast slain and hast redeemed us by thy blood"

(Revelation 5:9, 12-13). This is the plot of the tragedy; this is the crimson path that runs from the gateway of Paradise to the City of God.

And the singular fact is that the story, thus related with divine beauty, makes a personal appeal to every man. It needs to be so, since every man is conscious of sin, of a certain fearful anticipation of judgment, and of a desire to escape it. "What shall I do to be saved?" is the cry of the sin-cursed race. And here is where the gospel of the Bible finds us.

Let it be said with all possible emphasis that this scriptural plan of salvation stands solitarily and alone. There are other religions and other philosophies which undertake with more or less success to solve important problems and suggest plans of right living, but there is no religion or philosophy outside of the Scriptures which suggests a rational way to escape from the guilty past. All others are ineffectual at this point. Indeed, not one of the sacred books of the false religions gives the slightest hint or indication of any method of erasing the record of past sin. Here the Scriptures stand alone. We are saved by faith in the atoning blood, and without this shedding of blood there is no remission of sin.

And what shall be said of the central figure of this drama? Has the adverse criticism of the centuries robbed us of Christ? No; he remains by common consent the unequaled One. His name is *Wonderful.* Wonderful in his birth. Wonderful in his life, a life condensed in the brief thesis: *[He] went about doing good* (Acts 10:38). Wonderful in his death, as the infidel Rousseau said, "If the death of Socrates was that of a sage, the death of Jesus was that of a God!" And wonderful, surpassingly wonderful, in his influence through all the succeeding ages.

A hall of fame was recently dedicated in connection with one of our universities, and many illustrious names have been inscribed on its walls, but who would think of comparing any of them with Christ? A company of English writers was once discussing the relative greatness of the world's famous teachers. "If Plato or Socrates or Epictetus or Marcus Aurelius or Sakyamuni were to enter here," said Charles Lamb, "we would immediately uncover in their presence, but if Jesus of Nazareth were to appear, we would all with one consent fall upon our knees before him!"

In his exile Napoleon said, "My life once shone with the brilliance of a diadem, but now who cares for me? Caesar, Alexander, and I dreamed of a universal empire. Caesar and Alexander, where are they? And I shall soon be forgotten. But Jesus stretches a dead hand across the centuries and rules the world. He was crucified eighteen hundred years ago, after founding an empire upon love, and at this hour millions would die for him!" It is true that the glory of his name increases with the passing of the years. His praises are sung by a multitude whose voice is as the sound of many waters:

> All hail the power of Jesus' name!
> Let angels prostrate fall.
> Bring forth the royal diadem,
> And crown him Lord of all![36]

It is no marvel that a book with such a plot and such a Hero should have withstood the fiercest attacks of its bitterest foes. The "impregnable rock of Scripture," as Gladstone called it, stands like Gibraltar with the wreck of many hostile fleets scattered around its base. It stands like the Eddystone Lighthouse, despite all swirling tides and buffeting storms, casting a steady light for the guidance of perplexed mariners on dangerous seas. It stands and withstands, this round-tower of the King of Kings, while over it floats with ever-increasing splendor the red banner of the cross.

---

36   Edward Perronet, "All Hail the Power of Jesus' Name," 1780.

Chapter 20

Its Enemies

It is not claimed that the friends of the Bible are perfect, only that they are trying to adjust themselves to its demands. They know, far better than their severest critics, how far short they fall of the splendid ideal set before them. But they keep on trying like hill-climbers who make their weary way with much stumbling toward a palace on the distant heights. Thus, trudging on amid adverse judgments and with much confusion, they confidently hope for better things someday. Not counting themselves to have obtained as though they were already perfect, they forget the things which are behind and reach forth unto those which are before and press toward the mark for the prize of their high calling (Philippians 3:12-14). Theirs is no easy task (let those who think so try it), but the end crowns the work. *Eye hath not seen, nor ear heard, neither have entered into the heart of man, the things which God hath prepared for them that love him* (1 Corinthians 2:9).

So much for the friends of the Bible. On the other hand, who are its enemies? The Book stands willing to be judged by the enemies it makes. It is undeniable that among the enemies are many whose outward lives are beyond reproach. But it is equally undeniable that their faction includes all reckless and notorious evildoers, all notorious thieves and adulterers, all habitual liars and blasphemers, all Sabbath breakers, all midnight revelers. They include all willful opposers of law and order, all confirmed criminals, all incorrigible tramps and professional ne'er-do-wells. All these can, without fear of contradiction, be reckoned as enemies of the Bible. If an exception is to be found, it occurs so rarely and the exposure of its insincerity is so obvious that it confirms the rule.

But these are not all. Among the avowed or clandestine foes of Scripture are many who occupy honorable positions in society, places of authority in political life, college professorships, and even pulpits and theological chairs. They are scrupulous in their observance of all the common proprieties and conventionalities. The astute cleverness of a score of such respectable men is more disastrous to the faith of the unwary than the blasphemous murmurings of a legion of disreputables. Nevertheless, they do not prevail. God's Word has come to stay, and the gates of hell shall not prevail against it.

One of the provisions in the ancient code of Deuteronomy had to do with the preservation of fruit trees: *When thou shalt besiege a city a long time, in making war against it to take it, thou shalt not destroy the trees thereof by forcing an axe against them: for thou mayest eat of them, and thou shalt not cut them down (for the tree of the field is man's life) to employ them in the siege: Only the trees which thou knowest that they be not trees for meat, shalt thou destroy* (Deuteronomy 20:19-20).

Our purpose in this reference is to draw a parallel between the antibiblical critics of our time and those ancient destroyers of fruit trees. The world has always been divided into two hostile camps – defenders of the Bible and its enemies. The fiercest wars in history serve to illustrate this division, as in the Crusades where the clash of steel under the walls of Jerusalem was really a conflict between the Qur'an of the false prophet and the veritable Word of God.

This destroyer is always abroad in the land. No believer is allowed to rest in undisputed possession of any revealed truth. "The Reformer," written by the poet John Greenleaf Whittier (1846), is full of suggestion:

> All grim and soiled and browned with tan
>   I saw a Strong One, in his wrath,
> Smiting the godless shrines of men
>   Along his path.
>
> The Church, beneath her trembling dome,
>   Essayed in vain her ghostly charm:
> Wealth shook within his gilded home
>   With strange alarm. . . .
>
> Yet louder rang the Strong One's stroke,
>   Yet nearer flashed his axe's gleam;
> Shuddering and sick of heart I woke,
>   As from a dream.

It'd be well if this woodman had designs only on "the godless shrines of men," but unfortunately his axe is often laid at the root of the life-giving truths of our religion. He has invaded the Lord's orchard, despite the ancient rule of humanity in war, and the good trees, under whose shadow our fathers took delight and whose fruit was sweet to their taste, give back the echo of his blows. In this, however, there is no occasion for alarm. The war against the Scriptures is as old as the memory of man. Voltaire's words, uttered more than a hundred years ago, have often been quoted: "I will go through your theological forest and girdle every tree, so that in a quarter of a century not a sapling shall be left to you." Where now is that axe-man? But the forest is standing, and at last inspection, the Lord's trees were still *full of sap*. So Whittier continues:

> Take heart! The Waster builds again, —
>   A charmed life old Goodness hath;
> The tares may perish, but the grain
>   Is not for death.
>
> God works in all things; all obey
>   His first propulsion from the night:
> Wake thou and watch! the world is gray
>   With morning light!

The Bible is a tree of knowledge under which devout men sit to contemplate the great truths. If there is no standard of authority, there can obviously be no certainty to any truth. In search of the Golden Fleece, Jason had to be able to direct his sailing by the North Star, or else all would have been dead reckoning,[37] and his ship would have drifted at the mercy of the winds.

There are only three conceivable seats of authority as to spiritual things:

One is "the infallible church," but the church, divided as it is and speaking with diverse tongues, must prove its infallibility before any thoughtful man can accept it.

Another is the Bible, our "infallible rule of faith and practice." We have laid down an earlier premise that God (assuming that there is a God) would not leave his children without some sort of trustworthy revelation of his holy will. The Bible, as we have seen, claims to be such a revelation, saying of itself that it came by *holy men of God [who] spake as they were moved by the Holy Spirit* (2 Peter 1:21).

---

[37] *Dead reckoning* is an old maritime term used to describe navigation by using known initial position without the aid of celestial observations.

Now suppose the church and the Bible are both untrustworthy; what remains? The only other standard of authority is reason or the inner consciousness. But observe where this lands us: every man becomes an ultimate law unto himself. Could presumption further go? "I am Sir Oracle, and when I open my lips, let no dog bark!"[38] We have rejected the infallible church and the infallible Book, only to affix our faith to an infallible ego!

In any event, however, they say the Bible must go. This is the logical conclusion of the antibiblical criticism of these days.

Farewell, old Book! The relentless censor sits, like Jehoiakim, before the fireplace in his summer house, Bible on his knee and penknife in his hand, calmly mutilating the only reliable authorization of our Christian hopes. Hasn't it occurred to those "snipers," who from behind their pulpits and theological chairs are accustomed to aim ill-grounded propositions against the Scriptures, that however insignificant the effect on the impregnable rock, immortal souls are in the range of their poisoned darts? They have turned the rejoicing of many a weak believer into tears of hopeless doubt; they have taken from those who are abroad in the bleak wilderness of temptation their only weapon of defense: namely, *the sword of the Spirit, which is the word of God* (Ephesians 6:17).

Such axe-men are today the most zealous foes of Scripture. They do not depend upon the methods of open warfare. The troops of Ulysses are no longer hurled against the walls of Troy; it is the enemy in the belly of the wooden horse that menaces the city. The truth is no longer opposed with a challenge but with a rising inflection as in Genesis 3:1: *Yea, hath God said?* The argument is urged with a more or less equivocal and left-handed denial of the supernatural factor in both the written and the incarnate Word. Such a method of procedure is disingenuous,

---

38   William Shakespeare, *The Merchant of Venice*, 1598.

of course, and admittedly so, since in all common honesty, there is no serious effort to defend it.

This is precisely what Jesus foretold: *Many false prophets shall rise, and shall deceive many* (Matthew 24:11); and again: *Beware of false prophets, which come to you in sheep's clothing, but inwardly they are ravening wolves* (Matthew 7:15). The teaching of the apostles abounds in similar admonitions, as when Peter says, *There shall be false teachers among you, who privily shall bring in damnable heresies, . . . and many shall follow their pernicious ways; by reason of whom the way of truth shall be evil spoken of* (2 Peter 2:1-2). Therefore, the manifest duty of all Christians is to be on their guard, and of all Christ's ministers to speak plainly of the axe-men who subtly and treacherously oppose the truth.

To speak in this way is not intolerance, or else Christ and his apostles would not have led the way. Nor can it offend the faithful, since he who takes offense by putting on the garment pleads guilty by confessing that it fits him.

The false prophet, as Jesus says, may be known by his fruits, not merely by his moral misdemeanors but also by his way of putting things. The old-time infidel would have frankly thrown down his gauntlet in this way: "The Bible is a fraud, and Jesus is an impostor." But our modern strategist would command a large vocabulary of ambiguous words and phrases. One touchstone, however, will always betray him. He denies that God has truthfully revealed himself either in the Scriptures or by logical progression in Christ.

1. He will tell you that he believes the Bible, but pursuing the subject further, you discover that he is juggling with words. When he says, "The Bible is true," he means only that it is occasionally so. When he calls it the "Word of God," he means only that it is one of many such words. When he talks about

inspiration, he means simply an inspiration common to the world's literature. And when he ascribes divinity to Christ, it is the same divinity which he shares with all others who are created in the image of God.

If words were coins, such men would be liable to be arrested for counterfeiting; presumably they are thus liable in that appellate court where the term *honesty* is not restricted to commercial transactions but has to do with the secret imaginations of the hearts of men.

2. And if you still insist on the truthfulness of the Scriptures, this clever adversary will inquire with a lifting of his eyebrows, "Is your religion then the religion of a book?" To this we may safely answer, "Why not?" It is the religion of the Bible as the ultimate and only authority concerning Christ and his gospel. Suppose you ask him where he finds *his* standards of authority. If he rejects the Bible, which is the only accepted authority about Christ, his only alternatives are to take either an infallible church or an infallible ego. Out of this dilemma, no escape is possible except into the camp of the agnostics whose slogan is "I know not."

3. Then he will probably ask why you lay such emphasis on the question of whether Moses wrote the Pentateuch or not. And that will further disclose his utter disingenuousness, for nobody knows better than he knows that the question is not "Who wrote the Scriptures?" but "Are they true and trustworthy as coming from God?" The question is not as to the secretary who held the pen but as to the divine mind that moved it. It is indeed insignificant who wrote the Pentateuch or Isaiah or any other portion of the Scriptures, except as their authorship is definitely stated in the Bible itself. But it is of vital importance to know whether the claim that the Bible makes for itself

is correct or not: namely, that it was *inspired* (literally, God-breathed) and transmitted through holy men who were moved by the Spirit of God.

4. Next, this mask-wearer will ask, "What difference can a few unimportant mistakes make with the broad doctrinal and ethical teachings of Scripture?" There again he is disingenuous. In fact, he does not limit himself to "a few unimportant mistakes"; he really holds that Genesis is a compilation of myths and legends; Deuteronomy a wholesale forgery; the prophesies of no significant value, and the entire Bible a mingled tissue of truth and falsehood. It is not a question of infinitesimals but of wholesale essentials. It is not a question of specks in the marble of the Parthenon but whether there ever was a Parthenon, and if so, whether it was really built of marble or only of wood, hay, and stubble. The Bible as interpreted by such mischievous teachers is not the best of books, but if one hundred of the most reliable volumes of current literature were placed beside it, the critics themselves being the judges, they would regard the Bible to be the least trustworthy of them all.

5. You may then expect this ingenious, disingenuous arguer to inquire with an air of amazement whether you "really believe there are no mistakes in the Bible," to which you may safely answer, "There are no mistakes in the Bible; though there are mistakes such as might naturally be expected in the process of transference and translation in the King James Version and in other current versions." He may then be pretty certain to say, "Oh, you mean you believe in the inerrancy of the original writing. Did you ever see it? And what have we practically to do with it?" At this point, suppose you meet him with a similar question about the incarnate Word: "Did you ever see Christ?

Did any living person ever see him? Did you ever hear anybody say that he had ever seen him? Why then believe in him at all?"

Attention is again called to the singular parallel between Christ and the Scriptures: (a) They are both alike called *the Word of God;* (b) they are both theanthropic; that is, the divine and human are inextricably blended in their fabric but do not prevent their absolute truth and faultlessness; (c) both originals have vanished from sight, but they are transferred through succeeding ages only through the lives and labors of fallible men; (d) nevertheless, we believe in the unseen Christ, and thus believing, we *rejoice with joy unspeakable and full of glory.* For a similar reason we believe in the original writing of the Scriptures as it left the pens of those inspired men. Despite all errors in the transferring of the two Words, written and incarnate, they both exist today in such substantial perfection as to be profitable *unto every good work* and wholly effective in guiding and saving men.

6. "But," says the clever controversialist, "what difference does it make whether the historical and scientific parts of Scripture are true or not, as long as its doctrinal and ethical propositions are reliable? Isn't its purpose to save men?" The answer is plain: to say that the only purpose of the Scriptures is salvation is pure assumption. They were intended to be profitable in all things, so *that [a] man of God may be perfect, thoroughly furnished unto all good works.* And if they are not truthful in respect to science and history, what ground have we for committing ourselves to their spiritual guidance? *Falsus in uno, falsus in omnibus* (False in one thing, false in everything). If the truthfulness of your witness is successfully resisted, the only thing for him to do is to step down and out of the witness box. The Bible is not reliable in any way unless it is trustworthy in every way.

7. "But," continues our deceptive opponent, "this is a question for experts. The points at issue can only be determined by the most profound scholarship. Would you set yourself against all progress and advanced scholarship? Biblical critics are now engaged in their elaborate investigations, and it is necessary for the unlearned to patiently await their conclusions." Is there, then, no learning except the microscopic skill to split a hair or analyze a fly speck in the margin of the text? Or is there really a broader, deeper, higher, truer scholarship which can only be found in the secret place with God?

But suppose we take these men at their word and concede that wisdom will die with them. What are the "unshod people" to do meanwhile, whose souls are agonizing for a solution to the problems of eternal life? Must they suspend the great question: "What shall I do to be saved?" And how long are they to keep themselves in such suspense, hung up like Muhammad's coffin between heaven and earth? Haven't "experts" been discussing these questions since the foundation of the world? And with what result? No, gentlemen, the Bible is the Book of the people, and its salvation is intended for all sorts and conditions of men. "Where are the wise? Where are the disputers of this world? Hasn't God made foolish the wisdom of men?"

Specialists have their place; let them keep it. Our Lord's promise of the Holy Spirit – *he will guide you into all truth* (John 16:13) – was not addressed to doctors of divinity and theological professors only, but also to all his disciples. The Bible is removed by that promise from the exclusive province of expert scholarship and placed within the universal comprehension. Let those who are open and avowed enemies of the Word pour on their destructive acids and kindle their hostile fires; meanwhile, it behooves those who feel the just constraint of covenant vows to vindicate their loyalty to the Scriptures by approving and defending them. The people are themselves the jury in this case, as they were in the Lord's controversy on Mount Carmel where Elijah met the priests of Baal; their verdict was, *The* Lord, *he is the God* (1 Kings 18:39).

8. "But you are mistaken," says our friend the enemy, "in asserting that our purpose is destructive. It may be that incidentally the faith of some has been shaken, but whatever may have occurred in the past while we were clearing away the debris, we are now engaged in constructive work." So much the worse. You are right in your confession thus far; you have found many lame people walking with crutches, but since you persuaded them to throw away their Bibles, it is high time that you furnish some other support for their uncertain steps. But what do you propose? A new Bible? Yes, you tell us that under the clear blaze of your scholarship, the Bible has become "a new book." It is indeed a new book, full of errors on all points within the recognition of the senses, yet heralded by you as a trustworthy guide in matters beyond sight. The thinking world derides you. Is this the monument which you have been so laboriously constructing? Is this your *refuge from the storm, a shadow from the heat* (Isaiah 25:4)? A Bible without ground of confidence? A religion without the supernatural? A gospel without oracles? A Christianity without Christ? A salvation without blood?

9. "No, but we do not deny Christ," they say. "On the contrary, we insist on loyalty to Christ. Our whole system is Christocentric. Back to Christ!" But back to what Christ? To the Christ of the Bible which you renounce? To the Christ who affixed his authoritative seal to the so-called fables of the flood, Lot's wife, and Jonah in the whale's belly? To the Christ who called the Scriptures *truth* and never breathed a word or syllable against their absolute inerrancy? To the Christ who said, *Search the scriptures;* [not to disprove them but because] *for in them ye think*

ye have eternal life: and they are they which testify of me (John 5:39)? Or, in your process of "construction" are you giving the world a new Christ too? One of your leaders recently said from his theological chair, "The time has come for a restatement of the doctrine of Christ." *Timeo Danaos et dona ferentes* (Beware of Greeks bearing gifts). We may be pardoned for affirming that under the circumstances, it is not enough for you to say that you believe in Christ.

10. However, we are privately advised by certain of these teachers that the truths of the new theology are esoteric; that is, they are for private consumption and not to be declared on the housetops. Worse and worse! There are no Eleusinian Mysteries in the religion of Christ. *An highway shall be there, and a way, and . . . the wayfaring men, though fools, shall not err therein* (Isaiah 35:8). Didn't the Master say, *Except ye be converted, and become as little children, ye shall not enter into the kingdom of heaven* (Matthew 18:3)? The man "in holy orders" who confidentially asserts opinions which he dare not preach in the great congregation is false to his obligation to declare the whole counsel of God. More than that, he is a coward. If not, let him, in vindication of his manhood and his Christianity, stand in the open and, whether men will hear or resist, pronounce the truth without mumbling, fearless of consequences and indifferent to tenure of office, what the God whom he professes to serve has enabled him to understand.

We are sadly in need of two particular classes of men these days. On the one hand, we need infidels, outspoken infidels, who will take their places in the open and lift up their banners against Zion. What has become of the atheists of former days? Where are the brave scoffers who defied Jehovah and ran headlong on the ornamentation of his shield? Where is Goliath with his spear like a weaver's beam? Where are the fierce wolves of the wilderness? Alas, these are the degenerate days of wolves clad in sheep's clothing and mingling with the flock, of Doeg the Edomite skulking behind the altar, and of Shimei in ambush throwing stones at the king.

On the other hand, we need believers, out-and-out believers, who know the truth and dare to maintain it. There is no room for weak, middle-of-the-road men, or Redwalds with the motto *In utramque partem,* professing to stand on neutral ground while practically opposing themselves to Christ and the Scriptures. Everywhere the call is for men to follow him – men of conviction and courage to speak the last atom of truth, men who do not mince or mumble in their utterance but by faith proclaim, "These things we know." The call is for men who shine forth to the full measure of their light and withhold no truth that God gives them.

Chapter 21

Its Indestructibility

As far back as the memory of man runs, there has never been an hour of cessation in the attack upon the Scriptures as the Word of God.

The nineteenth century was ushered in amid a whirlwind of infidelity. In France the Reign of Terror had swept away all sanctions of the moral law. It was solemnly resolved in the Corps Législatif that "there is no God." The Sabbath was erased from the statute books. The friends of the French Encyclopédie were chanting requiems at the tomb of Christianity. All Europe followed the fashion. In our own country, religion was at its lowest ebb. As a matter of record, in the year 1800, there were only three professing Christians in Yale College. The author of *The Age of Reason,* in which were presented all the stock arguments against the inerrancy of Scripture, brought his manuscript to Benjamin Franklin for review. "Do not unloose this tiger," said Franklin; "for if our people are what they are with the Bible, what would they be without it?" But the tiger was unloosed. Paine and his colleagues appeared to have everything their own way. A tidal wave of unbelief swept over our country. It seemed as if the fountains of the great deep were broken up.

The twentieth century has begun in the same way. He is indeed a blind student of the past who does not perceive that Christianity has made magnificent progress, but every step of that progress has been bitterly and stubbornly contested. There is, however, a startling contrast between the former methods and those of today. The assault is now from within the gates. The open and avowed leaders of infidelity are gone. Bradlaugh in England and Ingersoll in America were the last of the Old Guard. Open warfare has given way to strategy. The Trojan horse has been wheeled within the walls of the church itself where a body of militant critics, many of them wearing the sacred garb of theological professors and ministers of the gospel, have been attempting to draw the bolts of the citadel. Here is a significant fact: there is not a fundamental truth of the Christian religion that has not been called into question and attacked by men in holy orders; that is, by men solemnly promised to uphold and defend those very truths. The objective of the assault is the integrity of the Holy Bible, now as much as ever, for it is rightly understood that if the citadel is to be overthrown, the city itself must fall.

What is the result? It might easily be supposed from the blowing of trumpets and beating of drums, and from the frequent claim that all scholarship is arrayed against the credibility of the Scriptures, that the Lord of the Scriptures had retired from the field. But he that sits in the heavens shall laugh. The thing that has been shall be. Despite the boastful prophecy of Voltaire, there are saplings still growing in the forest of God. A multitude of reverent scholars still stand for the ancient landmarks without trumpeting their achievements or blazoning them on the dead walls; an innumerable host of devout people are in no danger of being taken up by the lips of talkers. The Lord reigns and the citadel is safe. The heart of the universal church beats true to the inspiration and trustworthiness of the Word of God.

Let us observe how this continuous assault upon the Scriptures has affected their integrity if at all.

As to the scientific propositions of Scripture, enough has already been said, so that just a word here will suffice. It is claimed in some quarters, with much noisy shouting, that the leading scientists of recent times are all arrayed against the Bible. This can be conceded only on the assumption that a scientist becomes a "leading" scientist merely by virtue of his unbelief. Otherwise, the statement is denied *in toto*. What of Descartes and Locke? What of Sir Isaac Newton and Michael Faraday? What of Dana and Agassiz and Lord Kelvin? The last words of Professor Dana to the members of my class at graduation are worth repeating: "Young men, you are going out into a world where you must meet an unceasing assault upon your faith. Let me ask you to remember, as my parting counsel, that whenever you are in doubt amid the confused voices of scientific controversy, you may always with perfect confidence affix your faith to the statements of the Word of God."

The one proposition of the Scriptures which has challenged contradiction is its doctrine of origins: *In the beginning God created the heaven and the earth* (Genesis 1:1). To offset this, the doctrinaires have suggested a theory of evolution which is now asserted as "universally accepted." So far is this from being true that we may safely leave the defense of the evolution theory to scientists themselves, since it is most vigorously opposed in that quarter. Charles Darwin, headmaster of the guild, was frank to admit that evolution is still a mere hypothesis. We may be excused for insisting that under such circumstances the shout of victory on the part of those who deny the Mosaic narrative of the beginning is somewhat premature. The age-old view of the creation has not been nor can it ever be overthrown by guesswork. The guns that batter down the pyramids must be charged with other ammunition than the stuff that dreams are made of.

Nor have the efforts of the experimentalists met with any better success. They have much to say of autogenesis, or a beginning without God. As an old-fashioned believer, I am ready to surrender my faith in the biblical doctrine of origins as soon as one of these experimentalists shall create a single grain of sand. Surely, this is not too much to ask of men whose magic deals with worlds and universes. Let them produce a daisy or a caterpillar to begin with. Until some such result shall have been attained, we may be pardoned for standing by the old manifesto: *In the beginning God.*

The same is true of the assaults made upon the authenticity of the biblical records. Attention has already been called to this point. Suffice it here to say that not a single record of the slightest importance in the Pentateuch or other historical books of Scripture has ever been successfully impugned, but on the contrary, the researches of archaeologists are continually verifying them.

The theology of the Bible also stands as the valid philosophy of God. There are no atheists today. The infidelity of the last half-century has not busied itself in denying the true God so much as in making new gods. The pagan world has still its pantheon of idols formed of wood and stone, but lately civilized idolaters are industriously making gods out of the gray matter of their own fantastic brains. These are nonetheless idols, since they *have eyes, and see not; which have ears, and hear not* (Jeremiah 5:21). Any god except the God who has revealed himself in the Scriptures will suffice for a modern freethinker. Law? Force? Energy? The all-pervading soul of the universe, or "something not ourselves that maketh for righteousness"? What does it matter which of these you prefer? They are all specters: dull, senseless, inanimate things. In vain their devotees

ITS INDESTRUCTIBILITY

cry, "O Baal, hear us." There is no voice or answer or any that regard them.

> An immense solitary Specter stands!
> It hath no shape, it hath no sound,
> It hath no place, it hath no time;
> It is and was and shall be;
> It is never more nor less, nor sad nor glad;
> Its name is Nothingness!
> Power walketh high and Misery doth crawl,
> The clepsydron drips, the sands
> Fall down in the hour glass,
> And the hands around the dial sweep.
> The Specter saith 'I wait!'
> And at the last it beckons, and they pass.
> And still the red sands fall within the glass,
> And still the hands around the dial sweep,
> And still the waterclock doth drip and weep;
> And that is all![39]

The result is precisely what it was in ancient Greece; in the midst of innumerable shrines and statues stands an altar representing the consummate fruit of human wisdom, inscribed: "To the unknown God." And still from Mars Hill ring out the words: *Whom therefore ye ignorantly worship, him declare I unto you* (Acts 17:23). The God of the Bible remains as the only God who satisfies human need. He alone controls the destinies of nations and the children of men. He alone gives *beauty for ashes, the oil of joy for mourning, the garment of praise for the spirit of heaviness* (Isaiah 61:3). This is the God of the Scriptures, and there is none other beside him.

The ethics of the Scriptures are the judicial basis of civilization

---

39   Sumner Lincoln Fairfield, *The Siege of Constantinople*, 1822.

throughout the world. How much of its moral code has perished in the hot fires of the centuries? Not one jot or tittle of it!

Its singular plan of salvation is the only answer which has ever been suggested to the question, "How can a man be just with God?" The crux of the argument is the cross. It is the one supreme unanswerable guarantee of the endurance of the Scriptures as the inspired Word of God.

A century and a half ago, while visiting Paris, Lord Chesterfield was entertained at the table of a distinguished lady of the Encyclopédie. She said to him, "My lord, I am informed that your English Parliament is composed of five or six hundred of the most profound and brilliant thinkers. This being so, will you explain how it is that, under their authority, the Bible is still recognized as final authority in the legislation of your country, and how it is that the obsolete religion of the crucified Nazarene is maintained as your state religion?"

His answer was, "Madam, this is a mere temporary makeshift; we are casting about for something better, and when we discover it, the Bible and Christianity will certainly give way."

The world has been hunting during all these centuries for something better and has not yet discovered it. And the thing that has been, will be. Dreamers will still dream on; undevout thinkers will pursue their hopeless quest; kings and potentates will continue their search for a new and better religion as they have done by the light of Smithfield fires and the burning of heretics, but thoughtful and reverent men and women will go on loving their Bibles. The troubled will run for comfort to this shelter as to the shadow of a great rock in a weary land. Sinners will search the Scriptures for a clear hope of salvation and find it under the cross. For there is no weapon in the arsenal of unbelief that can prevail against the "Yea" and "Amen" of the living God.

Afterword

I have one more reason for maintaining and defending the truth of the Scriptures, and it is a purely personal one. Its value is set forth in a homely old proverb, which says, "The proof of the pudding is in the eating." No amount of argument on behalf of revelation – or of any other proposition, for that matter – will benefit those who decline to taste and see for themselves. Philip's argument with Nathanael as to the messiahship of Jesus reached its logical conclusion in the words, *Come and see.* God himself is practically nothing to one who refuses to contemplate him.

It is five and forty years since the writer, then a young theology student, found himself and his calling at the deathbed of a stranger. So long ago did the old Book "find me" (Thanks, Coleridge, for that word!), and never once in these five and forty years has it failed me.

1. The longer I live and the more familiar I become with the arguments for and against the trustworthiness of the Bible, the more firmly I believe it. A Christian who stands braced against "the impregnable rock" (Thanks, Gladstone, for that phrase!)

is not likely to be moved by a procession of players on instruments, trumpeting as they pass.

I have lived to see the former positions of the antibiblical critics abandoned, almost without exception, one by one. The new ground, which they now professedly occupy, is so far from being new that their campfires are kindled in the very ashpits left by Paine and Voltaire more than a century ago. But there is this difference: whereas the banners that floated over the old-time encampment wore the bold legend "We are infidels," they now read, "We are Christians." These foes of Scripture call themselves progressive. I too believe in progress, but because I have studied the singular habits of the hermit crab, I much prefer to call myself conservative. The comets, doubtless, as they whizz through infinite space with a freedom that knows no rhyme or reason, make sport of the planets that move contentedly in their ancient orbits; but what does it matter to the old-fashioned planets if they laugh last? The great body of believers in the universal church are progressive conservatives, moving on but never so rapidly as to exceed the speed limit as indicated by the progress of the pillar of cloud.

The advanced liberals are relatively few, but "behold what a great fire a little spark kindleth!" Not content to walk in sunlight, they propose to drive the chariot of the sun. To them the lesson of Phoebus is as meaningless as the "fables" of the Old Testament and the "myths and legends" of the New. I for one can see no reason for falling for their views. The company of those who "just know, and know no more, their Bibles true" is more congenial for any humble follower of Christ. He believed the Bible, knew it by heart, loved it, preached it, practiced it, commended it to his disciples as the means of evangelizing the world, and never once in all his ministry spoke a word or syllable against its absolute truth and trustworthiness. The Bible, which my Lord and Savior thus approved, is good enough for me.

AFTERWORD

I am not unaware of the difficulties that confront one who accepts the Bible with its presentations of spiritual truth. The problems which lie beyond the bounds of the five physical senses are not to be cut like Gordian knots. Their solution calls for the exercise of faith, a sixth sense with which man alone, in distinction from all the lower orders of life, has been equipped, so that he might comprehend the things which are unseen and eternal. But, *the carnal mind is enmity against God* and against all the truths that center in him (Romans 8:7). We are naturally averse to accepting what we cannot see and handle, hence the difficulty which always besets us in approaching the truths of the spiritual life.

Nevertheless, to my mind it is easier to accept the Scriptures as inerrant than to believe that a loving God would leave his bewildered children to wander in a world of confused voices without a trustworthy guide. No such guide is found in reason, in conscience, or in hierarchical infallibility of the so-called sacred books of the false religions. There are unimportant diversities and discrepancies in each of them. It is easier, incomparably easier, for one to believe that God did really and authoritatively speak through holy men who wrote *as they were moved by the Holy Spirit*, and that the Word thus written has been preserved by a special providence in essential purity as we now have it, than to believe in a God who would leave us to blunder through a labyrinthine life into the great unknown with no adequate effort to direct us along the way.

Now, allow me to speak more specifically of the three great doctrines of the Bible: namely, a personal God, holy, just, and good; a man with a divine birthright but fallen into sin and thereby alienated from God; and the God-man through whom an *at-one-ment* (atonement) is effected between God and man.

These three doctrines, containing the sum and substance of Scripture as set forth in the teachings of Christ, are subtly or admittedly denied by the advanced liberalism of our time. The personal God is reduced by liberals to an impersonal force which is scarcely the specter of a god. The man, then, whom the Scriptures represent as created in the likeness of God, was not created at all but evolved from the lower orders of life and, as the creature of heredity and environment, is an utterly irresponsible being. And the God-man is no God-man but a mere man posing as God and therefore powerless to save. Thus, the whole doctrinal system of the Scriptures is more or less politely abandoned out of doors.

This is frequently done by men in holy orders and under covenant vows. As an honest man, I do not like to contemplate this fact. As a man of average common sense, I am unable to understand it. As a Christian, I recoil from it. As a conservative, I find it easier to accept each and all of the great doctrines referred to than to reject them in the manner indicated, notwithstanding the mysteries involved in the necessity of the case.

In order to reject the God of the Scriptures, I would have to believe in effects without causes, in design without a designer, and in law without a lawgiver. However great my faith may be – or call it credulity, if you prefer – it is not equal to the strain thus put upon it.

In order to reject the scriptural doctrine of man, I would have to believe in a theory of evolution, which is truly a mere hypothesis, and in the irresponsibility of a being equipped with a sovereign will, and – without the scientific fact of dynamic conservation – in the possible extinguishing of the mightiest of known forces. My progressive friend, in the name of science I protest that I cannot keep up with you.

In order to reject the biblical doctrine of the God-man, I would have to affirm that Christ was either man alone or God alone. In the latter case, I must follow in the footsteps of the

AFTERWORD

Docetists[40] whose undefendable theory was exploded a thousand years ago. In the former case, I must face an impossible dilemma. For if Christ was a mere man, he must have been either a good man or a bad one. If he was a good man, how shall I account for the fact that he attributed to himself every one of the divine attributes, accepted the devotion due to God alone, and died for making himself equal with God? It is equally difficult to believe that he was a bad man, for the whole world pays tribute to his singularly blameless life and character. But we must believe something about him.

And there is no middle ground. He was either what he claimed to be, or he was a shameless impostor who was justly sentenced to die on the accursed tree.

In view of these facts, I say it is easier to believe in the Bible than to follow with those who reject it.

2. In looking back over these five and forty years, it is not enough to say that the Bible has forced itself on my confidence by its intrinsic reasonableness. I have seen it making men, and I have cherished the hope that it might ultimately build me up *unto the measure of the stature of the fulness of Christ* (Ephesians 4:13). My own many and most lamentable failures and shortcomings have served to emphasize its reliability as an infallible rule of faith and practice.

When Jesus said to his disciples, *Search the scriptures,* he went on to give them a good and sufficient reason for doing so: namely, because *in them ye think ye have eternal life: and they are they which testify of me* (John 5:39). He thus indicated that he himself is the secret of eternal life, and in my observation and personal experience, I have found him so. The measure of our success in the building of character is our intimacy with the incarnate Word as revealed in the written Word of God.

---

40 Those who believe that Jesus had no human body and only appeared to have died on the cross.

To neglect the Bible, then, is to invite leanness of soul. This Book is the lattice from behind which the Good Shepherd looks out upon the Shulamite maid (Song of Solomon 2:9). His promise to us is, *Lo, I am with you always* (Matthew 28:20), but there are times when our eyes are so hindered that we cannot see him. However, we can always catch the vision by opening the Bible. It is in the faithful and habitual searching of the Scriptures that we keep up an unbroken friendship and fellowship with him. The Rock upon which our faith fastens its anchor may be invisible, but laying our hand upon the anchor chain, we are assured by the throbbing of its mystic current that our faith is still secure, taking hold of that which is *within the veil* (Hebrews 6:19).

3. Nor yet, in looking backward, is it enough to say that I have believed the Scriptures and have endeavored to translate them into the terms of common life and character. It is only fair to add that, as a minister under bonds to *preach the word,* I have, in all good conscience, sought to commend it to my fellow men.

The temptations to do otherwise are deceptive and diverse. There is no lack of people with *itching ears* who go about from one sanctuary to another in search of preaching for the times (2 Timothy 4:3). And the newspaper announcements of church services indicate that they have no difficulty in finding it. The moralistic shoemaker who, instead of sticking with the trade, becomes a jack-of-all-trades, is certain to be master of none. His cornerstone of benefit is the Word. In art, science, and philosophy, he is only a novice at best, and when he ventures into politics, he is smilingly pitiful compared to those who make a business of it. The result of such poaching on alien preserves is usually not that preaching which is the power of God unto salvation, but the preaching of foolishness which neither saves nor helps anybody and has its labor for its pains.

But the minister who stands by his commission in the preaching of the Word is on his native ground. Assuming fair ability and reasonable industry, he will not lack for an audience, since the deepest longing in the soul of the average man is to know the way of salvation as indicated in the Scriptures. The people who come to church do not care particularly to hear what the preacher thinks about this, that, or the other thing, but they are deeply concerned about knowing the mind of God.

The prevailing passion for sensationalism has much to do with the decline of pulpit power today. All sorts of outside helps are resorted to in the effort to gain a hearing, as if an audience was worthwhile only for what the preachers can do with it. And the flying trapeze is sure to lose in the long run. The only sensationalism which is permissible in the pulpit is that which borrows its lightning from the bolts of heaven.

We profess to believe in God and we profess to believe in man divinely born and alienated from God. It is for us to paint sin so black that sinners, pricked to the heart, will be forced to cry, *Men and brethren, what shall we do?* (Acts 2:37). If Nathan the prophet had followed the custom, he would have closed his discourse with the parable of the little ewe lamb, and gone away with the congratulations of the king and his courtiers on having delivered a beautiful sermon. But the parable of the little ewe lamb was only the feather of a shaft that, flying from the prophet's bow, struck David in the region of the heart and sent him staggering to his closet in the housetop with the cry, *Lord, be merciful unto me: . . . for I have sinned against thee* (Psalm 41:4).

We profess to believe in Christ as the only Savior from the penalty and power of sin. Because of that belief, we preach the incarnation: *Great is the mystery of godliness: God was manifest in the flesh* (1 Timothy 3:16). We preach the atonement, pointing to the cross as Moses pointed the dying Israelites to the effigy of the brazen serpent with the cry, "Look and live!" We preach the resurrection, that is, life and immortality brought to light in him who, rising from the sepulcher in Joseph's garden, entered heaven on our behalf with the keys of death and hell at his girdle.

These are some of the truths which we are commissioned to preach. They open up from a thousand standpoints in infinite variety, but always point one way. Behold the cross! And Jesus said, *I, if I be lifted up from the earth, will draw all men unto me* (John 12:32). He is the great magnet. His is the drawing power. Is it sensationalism we want? The tragedy of his self-denying love in our behalf is the sensation of the ages.

What opportunities are here for chaining the attention and capturing the hearts of men! The Bible presents us with a quivering chain of sensations from beginning to end. Alas, the fault is ours! We preachers are so prone to dullness, and dullness in the pulpit is an unpardonable sin. What we need is not to lead our congregation into pastures new but to acquaint ourselves more intimately with the green fields that lie along the water of life. Lord, open thou thy Word to the shepherds of Israel!

So, in the experience of the years, the power of the Bible has increasingly taught me the truth of it. In this little volume, I have tried to give my reasons for believing it, for adjusting my life to it, and for preaching it. If a single reader is led to place a deeper and sweeter confidence in my Savior's Book, I shall be glad and happy.

Dear Bible! Book of the church militant and triumphant; Book that our fathers touched with reverent hands, and our mothers stained with grateful tears; Book that no bonfires have been able to consume or fuming acids to impair; Book of comfort for the sorrowing, of strength for the weary, of courage for the living, and hope for the dying; my Savior's Book and mine – if I forget thee, may my right hand forget its cunningness. If I fail to preach thee, may the living coal no longer kindle on my lips. May my tongue cleave to the roof of my mouth if I don't find thy saving truths my chief joy!

David James Burrell
– A Brief Biography

David James Burrell was born on August 1, 1844, the son of David and Elizabeth Burrell, and great-grandson of John Burrell, a French Huguenot who was driven from Alsace at the revocation of the Edict of Nantes in 1685. He immigrated to America and settled in the Mount Pleasant area of Pennsylvania.

The family lived in that area until 1851 when David's father's business partner fled with all the business funds. The incident rocked his father's faith in God and man. In those dark days, David's mother told a mischievous six-year-old David that it was in her heart for him to be a minister of the gospel.

In 1851, the family's "voyage" took them down the Monongahela River to the Ohio River to the Mississippi River to the Illinois River to north-central Illinois. After traveling seventy miles over land by following Indian trails through grass that was taller than the horses' backs, they reached Freeport, Illinois.

But the land that David's father had paid an option for had been claimed by another family, so they purchased and ran a supply store with barrels of pickles, sugar, and other goods.

Freeport settlers were mostly German, which also meant there were taverns with free-flowing beer.

After living in a hotel for a year, the family moved to a house across from the county jail. One day the constable showed David a dead man in order to convince him not to drink alcohol. David's father drank, but his mother did not. Seeing this man and watching his father turned David against liquor.

One day, however, a farmer caught David stealing watermelons. He took David to his house, tied him up with a clothesline, and told his wife he was taking him to the jail. David said, "I rode to town, bound with ropes, and in view of everyone." He was frightened with every nerve and fiber in his little body. Outside the jail, the farmer released David at his mother's door across the street. Though David vowed to kill the farmer, years later when they met, he shook his hand.

In high school, David excelled in composition and declamation. He participated in the debating and speaking society and had opportunity to hear great speakers such as Horace Greeley, Ralph Waldo Emerson, and Frederick Douglass.

In spite of excelling in these areas, David played hooky from school so often that he was taken out of school and put to work in a drugstore. But after a lawless venture with Mexican coins, he was sent back to school.

When the financial crisis of 1857 drew near, money was scarce, so David, age thirteen, became innovative. The *Rockford Daily News* needed a Freeport correspondent, and David applied and got the job – sight unseen. Every morning he wrote his "newsletter" and signed it "Stephenson." He wrote for two years incognito until he injected politics into his news. After an editor rebuked him, his sister discovered his identity and forced him to end his career as a society reporter.

During the political season of the 1850s, David's father took him to meet and shake hands with Abraham Lincoln. Later,

David attended the Lincoln-Douglas debate in Freeport on August 27, 1858, after which he maintained a love for Lincoln and studied his speeches and deliveries.

In 1860, David was sent to Phillips Academy at Andover, Massachusetts, to finish his prep for Yale. He experienced the wrath of the principal when he was caught smoking and playing euchre. He was placed under a guardian, but his notes from that time show that he felt rage, hate, contempt, joy, and aspiration. He was super-sensitive and homesick. Though he never heard a word of encouragement, he had contact with Harriet Beecher Stowe who wrote a personal note to him in one of his albums.

As David neared graduation, his eyes started to fail. Upon examination, he was told not to strain them by reading printed words. The strong-willed, imaginative young man graduated in spite of the problem.

David entered college life at Yale with the vision of studying law. He plunged into the societies and was active and belligerent in rushes, helping to maintain even the banned societies. He found pleasure in college politics and founded and edited the *Yale Pot-Pourri*. This became a source of revenue for him, along with peddling his books.

David had drifted from his spiritual foundation to the point that he practically ceased to pray. He loved a good time, a good story, and singing. After graduation from Yale in 1867, he traveled west with no thought of the ministry. He dreamed of courtroom drama and public debate, so he planned to go to Columbia Law School, but he faced the greatest struggle of his life when he went home for the summer of 1867. His mother was waiting for him and said, "Thank God, Davy, you'll be going into the ministry now."

Unwilling to hurt his mother, he had told her nothing of his plans to go into law. In her mind, he had been set apart from infancy. David's own comment was, "I was no party to the agreement." He found the ministry idea repugnant, but quickly realized his difficulty was with God, not his mother, because his faith was gone. Because he could not disappoint his mother, he resolved to go to seminary to see if his faith could be restored.

David enrolled in the Congregational Seminary at Union Park, Chicago, and roomed at Farwell Hall, the headquarters of Dwight L. Moody, whose enthusiasm greatly influenced him. After his year at Union Park, David went to Union Theological Seminary in New York. Then he was offered a probationary superintendent's position at a mission on Sixth Avenue and given three Sundays to keep order. If he succeeded, he could stay. Two weeks produced pandemonium. With one week left, David instructed his organist to play no matter what; when chaos began, he grabbed the troublemaker by the collar and dragged him to the platform. After a physical brawl where David received teeth marks on his calf, he managed to subdue the troublemaker and force him to admit to everyone that David could thrash any of them; the school thrived in spite of David's doubts about his own faith.

That changed one night when one of the mission boys came for him. His father was dying but had drifted away from the Savior. All night long David sat by the bed to answer questions. "Tell me how to face God." "Is there a God?" "Can his blood cleanse me from all sin?" More questions were asked and answered until David's own faith was restored. He stated, "In trying to tell a sinner how to die, I found out how to live." Through his mission work, David's doubts were dispelled, and his faith strengthened, and work became a delight.

In 1870, David returned to the Chicago mission field. At the Third Presbyterian Church, he profited from his New York experience – simply "get the crowd, keep things moving, and preach the simple gospel." The poor came, and the mission grew. Then, the night before the Great Chicago Fire, a smaller fire wiped out the mission and most of the church, and the next day the Great Fire erupted. When David was able to get out, he traveled from the south side to the river, then to the north side. The roads were clogged with vehicles, people, and furniture. He drove down the west-side bank of the river and saw piles of smoking ruins across the river. He heard explosions and saw flames still roaring in the north and south.

A week later, David Burrell married Clara DeForest. Soon after, David was ordained by the Presbytery of Chicago and installed as a minister of Peoria Street Chapel, which later became the Westminster Presbyterian Church. During his years in Chicago, David fought against the liquor traffic and preached against the red-light district. While Westminster prospered, David was still an assistant pastor and yearned for a church of his own, so he accepted a call from Dubuque, Iowa, where he served from 1876 to 1887.

Because David preached against breaking the Sabbath, liquor traffic, and gambling, the newspapers ridiculed him. Dubuque was a brewing center in the Midwest, so there were many beer gardens and saloons there. It was a city focused on politics, education, and alcohol, which caused the saloon crowd to hang him in effigy on July 4.

During this turbulent time, the eldest Burrell daughter, Miriam, became ill and died. David's depth of grief led him to a ministry for sorrowing people. He learned to comfort and visit the sick and sorrowful, but due to fatigue and the pressures involved, he was forced to take time away.

Upon returning to Dubuque in 1887, he accepted a call from Westminster Church in Minneapolis. The previous decade had been one of growth and development, so David was at his prime. He had a strong appeal to thoughtful, professional men because he gave solid meat in his sermons. With increasing effectiveness, he maintained a single theme and used powerful illustrations.

Sometimes David Burrell stirred up public interest before his sermon by reading for five minutes on an issue. But having resolved to never preach without a challenge to accept Jesus Christ as Savior, his emphasis was evangelism and defense of the faith. He preached without notes and with a rich, clear voice.

In 1891, Marble Collegiate Church, Reformed Dutch, in New York, called David to be their pastor. Though he had declined twice before, D. L. Moody convinced him to consider the opportunity. When the search committee agreed to everything he wanted, he accepted. Marble Collegiate Church was in the center of the hotel and apartment district.

David's first sermon was from John 3:16, but he was disappointed with the sparse attendance. He closed the church for the summer and renovated the building. He moved the lectern to the side and the choir to the front. He connected the great organ to four smaller ones – all to be played by one keyboard. His senior assistant ministered to the youth, and the second assistant canvassed the area of transient people. Young and old flocked in to hear the old gospel with a new, hometown friendliness.

David was disciplined with his sermon preparation, working every morning from outlines he prepared through summer months. Then he printed his sermons to stimulate attendance. He sold subscriptions to the *Marble Collegiate Pulpit* and used the funds for copies to shut-ins in jails, hospitals, and the military.

David Burrell fought the liberal trends in the church, which earned him the title of "bigot"; he chose conservatism in church doctrine, preaching against entertainment and working on the Sabbath. David remained connected to the Marble Collegiate Church for the rest of his life.

One of the happiest experiences of his life was his work with the students at Princeton Theological Seminary. For eight years, first as acting professor of homiletics and later as professor-elect, he reveled in training the boys.

In 1905, David became one of the seven incorporators of the Anti-Saloon League of New York State, and later served as its director from 1921 to 1923. In 1923 his health forced him to retire.

David's positions in his final decades included president of World's Council of the Reformed and Presbyterian Churches (1909–1913); summer preacher at Moses Taylor Memorial Church in New Jersey; member, then chairman, then vice president of the publishing committee of the American Tract Society; trustee of the United Society of Christian Endeavor; trustee of the Presbyterian Hospital in New York; president of Phillips-Andover Alumni Association (1917–1918); associate editor of *The Presbyterian, The Philadelphia (Evening) Herald,* and *The Christian Herald;* and president of the General Synod of the Dutch Reformed Church (1920).

In addition to these many responsibilities, David Burrell authored forty books. After a few months of failing health, David preached his last sermon in March of 1926. Later that year he prayed for the Lord to use him, then take him home, which he did on February 5, 1926.

Other Similar Titles

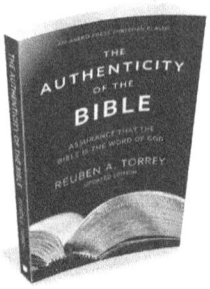

The Authenticity of the Bible, by Reuben A. Torrey

All scripture is given by inspiration of God, and is profitable for doctrine, for reproof, for correction, for instruction in righteousness. – 2 Timothy 3:16

Is the Bible the Word of God? That is the most important question for humanity. If the Bible is the Word of God, if it is an absolutely trustworthy revelation from God Himself, of Himself, His purposes, and His will, of man's duty and destiny, and of spiritual and eternal realities, then we have a starting point from which we can proceed to the conquest of the whole domain of religious truth.

This book will show you the absolute trustworthiness of the Bible. Follow the Word of God, and it will lead you as it has led thousands of others. It will lead you out of the uncertainty and the restlessness and the ultimate despair of unbelief and into the certitude, the joy, the victory, and the ultimate glory of an intelligent faith in the Bible as the Word of God, and in Jesus Christ as the Son of God.

Available where books are sold.

Surprised by Faith, by Dr. Don Bierle

The world is changing so rapidly that many are shaken with uncertainties. This is compounded by an erosion of confidence in absolute truth and traditional values. The result is a floundering search for a reliable source of purpose and meaning in life. *Fear, not anticipation, fills some hearts as people think about the future.* Some contend that turning to faith is anti-intellectual. "God is about religion," they say, "a crutch for the weak." These are mere caricatures resulting from ignorance. This book confronts false stereotypes and examines the astonishing body of scientific and historical evidence supporting the truth that *God exists and cares about people's future.* This is the Gospel *with evidence.*

Available where books are sold.

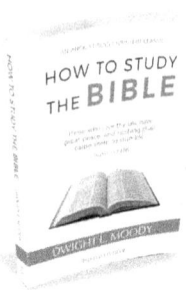

How to Study the Bible, by Dwight L. Moody

There is no situation in life for which you cannot find some word of consolation in Scripture. If you are in affliction, if you are in adversity and trial, there is a promise for you. In joy and sorrow, in health and in sickness, in poverty and in riches, in every condition of life, God has a promise stored up in His Word for you.

This classic book by Dwight L. Moody brings to light the necessity of studying the Scriptures, presents methods which help stimulate excitement for the Scriptures, and offers tools to help you comprehend the difficult passages in the Scriptures. To live a victorious Christian life, you must read and understand what God is saying to you. Moody is a master of using stories to illustrate what he is saying, and you will be both inspired and convicted to pursue truth from the pages of God's Word.

Available where books are sold.

The Importance and Value of Proper Bible Study,
by Reuben A. Torrey

There has perhaps never been an age that set such great store in study as that in which we now live. The unfortunate thing about it is that so much of the study in our day is devoted to books and subjects in which there is little or no profit. Time is squandered on the purely speculative, the uncertain, the unprofitable, the unessential, the unproductive, the irrelevant, and the transitory. The most profitable of all study is wisely ordered Bible study. Its value is incalculable. It is beyond all comparison more profitable than any other study. It is the one superlatively profitable study.

Available where books are sold.

www.ingramcontent.com/pod-product-compliance
Lightning Source LLC
Chambersburg PA
CBHW070140080526
44586CB00015B/1770